GHOST STORIES

of the

MARITIMES

Volume II

Vernon Oickle

GHOST
HOUSE

Ghost House Books

The Publisher: Ghost House Books
Distributed by Lone Pine Publishing
10145–81 Avenue
Edmonton, AB T6E 1W9
Canada

Website: http://www.ghostbooks.net

National Library of Canada Cataloguing in Publication Data
Oickle, Vernon L.
  Ghost stories of the Maritimes, volume II

  ISBN 1-894877-01-2

  1. Ghosts—Maritime provinces. 2. Legends—Maritime provinces. I. Title.
GR113.5.M37O322 2002   398.2'0971505 C2002-910571-4

Editorial Director: Nancy Foulds
Project Editors: Shelagh Kubish, Chris Wangler
Illustrations Coordinator: Carol Woo
Production Coordinator: Jennifer Fafard
Cover Design: Gerry Dotto
Layout & Production: Jeff Fedorkiw
Photo Credits: Every effort has been made to accurately credit photographers. Any errors or omissions should be directed to the publisher for changes in future editions. The photographs in this book are reproduced with the kind permission of the following sources: Susan Corkum-Green (p. 19); Lori Errington (p. 38); Paul Darrow (p. 56); Gerry Oram (p. 66); Tourism Nova Scotia (p. 84); Ann Brennan (p. 107); the Cumberland County Museum and Archives (p. 149); Tourism Cape Breton (p. 188); Lighthouse Publishing Ltd. (p. 140); Vernon Oickle (p. 61, 76, 95, 133, 163, 185).

The stories, folklore and legends in this book are based on the author's collection of sources, including individuals whose experiences have led them to believe they have encountered phenomena of some kind or another. They are meant to entertain, and neither the publisher nor the author claims these stories represent fact.

We acknowledge the financial support of the Government of Canada through the Book Publishing Industry Development Program (BPIDP) for our publishing activities.

PC: P6

Dedication

To the memory of my dearly departed sister, Heather

Contents

Chapter 4: Wandering Women

Chapter 5: Local Legends

Chapter 6: Maritime Mysteries

Chapter 7: Forerunners and Premonitions

Acknowledgements

After completing my first book of Maritime ghost stories for Lone Pine Publishing, I breathed a deep sigh of relief. It's a major challenge to conduct research, interview sources, decipher information and then write a book. So when the folks at Lone Pine asked if I'd consider writing a second volume of Maritime ghost stories, my first thought was to say no. After searching throughout Nova Scotia, New Brunswick and Prince Edward Island for tales for the first volume, I thought the task of finding sufficient material for yet another book would be insurmountable.

Thankfully, I was wrong.

Living in the Maritimes, I should have realized the wealth of material that exists in the oldest region of Canada. With hundreds of years of history and tradition to draw from, the search was not as difficult as I first had imagined it would be. However, it must be pointed out that volume two, like the first collection of ghost stories, would not have happened were it not for the generous support of many, many people throughout the region. These people told me their stories and pointed me in the direction of new sources for stories. I believe that with the support of these people, I have assembled an interesting collection of stories that is astounding, mystifying, enlightening and frightening.

It is appropriate then to acknowledge the people who were the sources of the incredible stories you are about to read and enjoy: Ann Brennan, Wilfred Fralic, David Goss, Marilyn Atwood, Jeff Clark, Donna Maquire, Elaine Bruff, Jay Remer, Darrell Dexter, Gordon Hansford, Shirley Chesley, Annabel and Ralph Rafuse, Vern Bagley, Roger Mahar, Yvette and Rick Henneberry, Susan and Ron Lane, George Munroe,

Glenn Coolen, Gary Selig, Iva Clayton, Jim Howe, Audrey Doane, Conrad Byers, Valerie Evans, Joan Helyar, Gerry Oram, Carl Trickey and Charles Rhindress.

In addition to these people, there were several sources who, while they would tell their stories, would do so only on the condition that they remain anonymous. As a storyteller, it is my job to tell these stories and not question the wishes of these people. The last thing I would want is to make these people feel uncomfortable because of this book. For that reason I have respected their wishes. However, their stories are still worth telling. I am confident you will shake your head in amazement.

Apart from the people who were the sources of these stories, many others played key roles in the making of this book. My colleagues in the community newspaper industry, Susan Corkum-Green and Lori Errington, assisted with several photos, as did photographer Paul Darrow. In addition to helping collect stories, Audrey Doane proofread the entire manuscript, an effort I greatly appreciate. The folks at the Cumberland County Museum and Tourism Nova Scotia were also helpful. And, as with my previous experience with Lone Pine Publishing, Nancy Foulds, Shelagh Kubish, Chris Wangler and the rest of the team were supportive and helpful in this endeavour. I thank them for all their help and guidance. I hope to work with them again some day.

Finally, as always, I save my last and biggest thank-you for my family, who have stood beside me as this book came together. No author can undertake such a task without the support and love of his or her family. I am blessed to have Nancy, Kellen and Colby in my corner.

Introduction

One of the first and most common questions I am asked about the stories in these books is if I believe what people tell me. Can all of this be true? the skeptic asks.

My typical and, some might say, sarcastic response is why not?

When I began researching and writing material for this second volume of Maritime ghost stories, I began with one simple promise to myself. I made a commitment that no matter what people told me, or how far-fetched it might seem, I told myself that I would not judge the material. That is not my job. As the author of these books, it is my responsibility to collect the material and to present it in a manner that is interesting and enjoyable to read. As for making the judgment call on whether the stories are true or embellished products of someone's over-active imagination, that is up to you to decide.

As a Maritimer myself, however, I will caution all the skeptics out there who may rush to judge. While I cannot say that I have personally experienced everything I write about in this volume of the paranormal, the mysterious and the unexplained, I can tell you that I have had my own experiences which have left me shaking my head and asking, how can that be? I can also tell you that when I look into the troubled faces of those people who share their stories and when I hear the emotional voices of people who sometimes speak in a whisper, I know that they believe what they say is the truth. Who am I to question their integrity? As the reader, you must try to keep an open mind about these things and remember that there are things in this world that defy simple explanations.

Although I have assembled an array of seemingly unbelievable stories, I invite you, the reader, to step into the magical, mysterious world of the paranormal. If you can suspend your pre-conceived notions and beliefs, and if you are willing to accept that there just may be something beyond this "real" world as we know it, then you will enjoy these stories. And when you finish the journey, you too will shake your head and ask, how can that be?

If you do that, and I think you will, then I have achieved my goal as collector and storyteller. If you are satisfied by the end of this voyage into the supernatural, then I have upheld my end of the bargain.

So, if you dare, find a quiet place somewhere in a secluded corner of your home, curl up in a comfortable chair with a warm blanket and turn the lights down low. And, as one of our upcoming tellers of tales will remind you, beware of things that go bump in the night...you just never know who—or what—might be there in the dark.

Happy haunting.

1
Haunted Houses

The Ghost in the Caretaker's House

Annapolis Royal, Nova Scotia, population approximately 700, is one of the oldest communities in Canada. Its many significant landmarks, including Fort Anne and Port Royal, are testament to the community's role in Canadian history. With its centuries of history, it's not surprising to find a few ghosts roaming the stately homes, historic structures and rolling hills of the quaint town. Local resident Iva Clayton knows all too well the connection between history and haunting.

From 1962 to 1968, Iva, her husband and their young daughter lived in the caretaker's house on the grounds of historic Fort Anne. Built in 1955, the modest two-storey house had a living room, dining room, kitchen, three bedrooms, a bath and a hallway. It was built to house a permanent caretaker who would look after the important landmark. Iva recalls they were happy to move into the house and even after some of their unusual experiences there, she still has fond memories of the place.

"We lived there for over six years," she says. "We had many happy times there—and we had some strange experiences. But through it all, I never felt threatened or concerned for ourselves in any way. In fact, there were only a few times when I felt scared—and those were whenever I was in the basement."

Iva recalls that the strange phenomenon began shortly after they moved into the home in the fall of 1962. "Several times during the day, when our daughter was just a baby, I'd be rocking her in the living room and I could hear people walking in the attic. I could also hear soft music, like a choir singing, from up there. Oftentimes I'd call my husband at work and say, 'Would you please come home and look in the attic because there's something going on up there?' He would do that from time to time. He'd come home, go up in the attic and have a look around. Each time he'd come back down and say, 'There's nothing there.' He'd look everywhere, but he could never find anything. But I know what I heard. I heard people moving about and people singing."

At some point after Iva heard the noises in the attic, other strange things happened. "It started that I'd put something down, say maybe in the bathroom on the counter. Then I'd go back for it, and it would be gone. Eventually, I'd find it some place else in the house—some place I would never think to put such objects. It would move from one place to another, sort of like it was playing with me, I guess."

Other times, Iva says, she and her husband would hear unusual sounds at night throughout the house. Sometimes they couldn't explain what the sounds were, but other times they could identify the origins of the sounds.

"Often at night we would hear the kitchen cupboard doors opening and closing," she explains. "I didn't mind it in the least. I wasn't a bit afraid of it. I never felt threatened. There were times that I'd even stay alone in the house while my husband travelled for his job. I'd hear the cupboard doors a lot at those times and when I heard them I'd say, 'If you can find something in there you can have it, so help yourself.' "

Perhaps, Iva says, that was just her way of coping with the possibility of living with a ghost. And there were times, she adds, that she did feel apprehensive or uneasy. "Of all the things that happened in that house, the only thing that I was really afraid of was going in the basement by myself. I'd always wait until my husband was home before I'd go down there and I'd often make him go with me. I'm not sure what it was, but sometimes while I was down there, I found that if I turned my head a certain way or turned around quickly, I'd see some sort of black shadow going through the air. It didn't last long, but I'd see it."

Iva recalls having a similar experience one night after going to bed.

"The street lights were right outside our house. They would illuminate the interior of the house so you could walk around at night without having to turn on any of the lights. I had a habit of changing our furniture around quite often. On this particular night, I had changed the bedroom furniture around so that I could lie in the bed and look out into the hallway. The bathroom was at the end of the hallway," Iva recalls. "On this night, my husband was in the bathroom getting ready to come to bed. I had already turned in and I was just lying there not really thinking of anything in particular."

Suddenly, Iva says, she heard a voice calling out to her and saying her name.

"It was just like something was calling my name. From where I was lying, I had to turn around to look at the bedroom door and when I did I saw something I hadn't been expecting. The doorway was filled with a presence. I don't know who or what it was, but there was definitely something there. It seemed to be a man because it was big and broad. And it seemed like it was wearing a white shroud of some sort and was holding his hand out to me. At first I thought it might be my husband and I remember thinking that if he was trying to frighten me, he was doing a good job of it. Then I realized I could see through it. I knew what it was."

Iva immediately yelled for her husband to come quick.

"When he heard me scream, he opened the bathroom door. Whatever was standing in the bedroom doorway quickly disappeared. We never had any idea or explanation as to what it was that night."

While Iva seemed to be the most sensitive to whatever force was in their house, she says her husband also had a few experiences of his own.

"This happened one night after we had gone to bed. You know the noise a blind makes sometimes when you pull it down and it slips and goes up and flops around? That's exactly the kind of noise we heard in the kitchen," Iva continues. "My husband got up and went to the kitchen to have a look around, but he couldn't find anything. We could hear it, but there was nothing there and everything was in its place. He thought that one of my blinds had slipped. He didn't know what to say when I told him we didn't have blinds in the kitchen. We never could explain the noises."

Although Iva and her family had many strange experiences in the house, she said she had some regrets about having to move out. "After we left, another chap and his wife moved in. I never told them anything about our experiences or about the house. One day, I was talking to the fellow's wife and I said, 'What do you think of the house?' She said, 'I love it.' But she also said, 'I'll tell you, though, I won't go down in the basement by myself.' I said, 'Oh, and why not?' She said, 'No way. I break out in goose bumps down there. There's just something down there I don't like.' "

Although Iva says they've never heard of anything out of the ordinary connected to the house that might explain the strange phenomena, she also believes that, given the historic nature of the property, it is possible that something may have happened on that spot at some time in the past.

But who knows? she asks. To her, it's all a mystery and some mysteries defy easy explanations.

The Man Upstairs

Annabel Rafuse of Milton, Nova Scotia, considers herself a God-fearing woman. The wife, mother and grandmother has been a vital member of her family and an active worker in her church all her life. She takes great pride in the contributions she has made to her community. She readily embraces her faith, giving herself freely to the glory of God and accepting that there must be something beyond this world as we know it. And with that, she quickly admits, she also believes in ghosts.

When she was seven, Annabel saw what she believes was a ghost. The experience has affected her throughout her life. At the time, her family lived in a homestead not far from where Annabel lives today. She recalls the event, she says, just as though it happened yesterday.

"I was seven and my brother, Ted, was a year younger. We were both sleeping in the same bedroom [one of four rooms in the family home]. We had gone to bed for the night and everything seemed normal."

Before this particular night, Annabel had never experienced anything unusual in the house.

"Anyway, when we went to bed, we snuggled down and went to sleep."

Some time later, she says, for some reason she awoke from her sleep and was startled to see, hovering at the foot of her bed, a man dressed in white and sporting a long, flowing beard and long hair. "He was just floating there with his hands stretched out, like he was reaching out to me. It was bright, like he was glowing…I just wanted to get out of there."

Annabel quickly slid from her bed, went to Ted's bed and woke him up. Together, the two youngsters made their way down the stairs and went to tell their mother about what they had just seen. "I don't think we felt threatened or anything like that. But we were only kids and naturally we were scared."

Over the years, as she talked to family members about the apparition she saw, she learned that others had seen a similar vision in the same house. "Back then, when older people began to lose their minds, it was normal to put them in rooms away from other people. They probably had Alzheimers disease or something like that, but in those days, we had not heard of such a thing. Many people said that my great-great-grandfather had gone a little crazy and that they had locked him in the basement. When he died, they said, his spirit stayed in the house."

Based on Annabel's description of the apparition she'd seen, her mother and other family members believed it was the ghost of her great-great-grandfather that had visited her that night.

Whatever, or whoever, it was, Annabel says she never again slept in the upstairs bedroom. From that night on, she slept on a small cot in the kitchen.

Mr. Holden Comes Home

Tourist promotions describe Lunenburg as one of Nova Scotia's most beautiful and historic towns. It was settled in 1753 by German and Swiss Protestants under British patronage, and these early settlers turned to the sea for their livelihood. Lunenburg became a world-class fishing and shipbuilding port, known far and wide as the home of the *Bluenose,* the schooner depicted on the back of the Canadian dime.

In 1995, the United Nations Educational, Scientific and Cultural Organization (UNESCO) designated "Old Town" Lunenburg as a World Heritage Site "because of the intactness of its British colonial model town plan, its pristine 18th and 19th-century wooden architecture and its long association with the fishing industry." Lunenburg is one of only two urban districts in North America to have this distinction. Today, Lunenburg is a vibrant fishing community, hosting many cultural festivals and events.

It is also home to many ghosts, one in particular that resides at 49 Cornwallis Street.

The home's owner, George Munroe, explains that the property is known locally as the Fink-Holden House. George says the house, built in 1829, has some interesting features besides its ghosts. "Mr. Fink had five daughters and was very protective of them. He felt the young men in the house next door were peeping Toms and were spying on his precious daughters. He boarded up all the windows on the east side of the house and you can still see where they were covered up. When the house was renovated seven years ago, and they took off some of the inside walls to put in insulation, there were the windows. It was quite amazing."

Before moving into the house in 1995, George says he never heard that the place was haunted. "There was never any talk about it being haunted or about ghosts. I would have paid close attention, since I've been a collector of ghost stories most of my life. I find them most intriguing."

George lived in the house for several months but did not experience any strange phenomena until February 1996.

At the time, George was staying in Halifax and some friends were staying at the house, taking care of things for him. "They were in the master bedroom. It's a lovely room, big and cozy. My guests were comfortable there. But things were different after that February night."

His friends reported that they were fast asleep when, at about two in the morning, the closet door burst open with enough force that it chipped the paint as it hit the wall.

"Of course there was no logical explanation for that. They told me the door had been closed tightly. But what could have forced it open with such a force?"

George has his own theories about that.

A few days later George was reading the obituaries in the provincial daily paper and noted the obituary for the last surviving member of the Holden family from Lunenburg, a man who at one time had lived in George's house. He found it particularly disturbing that at some time on the night in question, the man had died.

"I truly believe that the opening of that door was the old man returning to his house," George theorizes. "Since then, some nights when I wake up I have this weird feeling that somebody is in the house with me, but I have never been able to find anyone or anything."

George is adamant that his house is now haunted, but he takes it all in stride.

49 Cornwallis Street in Lunenburg, Nova Scotia, where a deceased former owner still lives.

"I've seen some pretty strange things, but I never feel threatened in any way. For example, it's not unusual now to see things move about the house on their own steam. One evening, I was sitting in the large chair in the living room. Out in the hallway, I had a small table with a piece of Trenton glass, a fruit bowl, on it. The piece was a very rare antique, about 120 years old, and it had belonged to my great-grandmother. All of a sudden, that dish shot off the table with enough force that when it hit the floor it smashed into a zillion pieces. It left grooves on the edge of the table where it went over. It actually gouged the table, that's how much force there was."

George says there is no rational explanation for this occurrence. He says the dish moved as if someone had picked it up and hurled it to the floor. But while he was upset that he had lost the priceless family heirloom, he still insists that he was never frightened. "I don't think this fellow means me any harm. He's just being mischievous."

George says he recalls waking up one night to the feeling that a presence was in the house. Going into the kitchen where he had the table set for breakfast the next morning, he found another strange phenomenon. "The table was still set, but it was now perfectly reverse from what I had done before going to bed. That's the kind of things he does—playful but not threatening."

George continues to refer to the ghost as a male because he is convinced that his mischievous visitor is the spirit of the last Holden family member. "I think it's only natural that it would be him. The family lived there for a very long time. When he got older, he had to leave, but after his death, I think he found his way back to the place that he loved so much."

Footsteps on the Stairs

Somewhere on Prince Edward Island there is a house reputed to be haunted. While the present occupants will tell the story, they ask that neither their identity nor the location of the house be revealed. Their concern, real or imagined, is that people will judge them to be crazy or, worse, decide their story is made up. However, they insist that the following story is true.

The house where these incidents are said to have occurred is on a beach very close to the ocean. The events began late in the 1970s, shortly after the family of four moved into their home. Let us say the family consists of a father, whom we shall call "Greg", a mother we'll call "Sandy", a four-year-old daughter named "Rebecca" and a six-year-old boy named "Matthew."

Three days after the family moved into their 80-year-old two-storey home, the first of many disturbing and unexplained happenings occurred.

Sandy recalls that just before noon on an August day, as she was making her way to the second floor, she discovered a set of wet footprints coming in the front door and going up the stairs. Since the footprints were small, Sandy concluded that Matthew had been in the ocean and had come into the house without wiping his feet. She went to her son's room and confronted him with her concerns. She told him that if he was playing in the water, he was to make sure he was dry before coming into the house. More importantly, he was not to be around the water unless his mother or father was with him.

"But Mommy," the little boy insisted, "I wasn't outside. I've been in my room."

Sandy dismissed the boy's comments as an attempt to protect himself from trouble. She insisted that Matthew promise to stay away from the water. Despite his continued insistence that he had not been near the water that morning, he finally gave in to his mother's demands.

The incident was quickly forgotten as the family went about unpacking and getting settled into their home—that is, until the next day when Sandy once again found a set of wet footprints taking the same path.

As she rushed up the stairs towards Matthew's bedroom, her son's promise from the previous day flooded into her memory. That he would break his promise so quickly did not sit well with Sandy. She was very upset.

When she confronted the boy, her anger rushed to the surface. As the mother scolded her son and lectured him about the dangers of the water and the seriousness of telling lies, Matthew tried in vain to explain that he had not been near the ocean.

Sandy did not accept his argument. Because Rebecca had been with her all morning, Sandy concluded that the small footprints belonged to Matthew. She told him he was not to leave his bedroom for the rest of the day and when he did leave the room, he must be prepared to apologize for lying and for breaking his promise.

The issue was closed as far as Sandy was concerned. It was important that her son understand the importance of keeping promises and obeying the rules as set down by his parents. Upon hearing the story from his wife, Greg attempted to speak with Matthew, repeating Sandy's concern and underlining the importance of staying away from the ocean. Greg and Matthew had always had a special bond. He believed Matthew would tell him the truth. Much to his surprise and dismay, however, the boy again insisted that he had not been near the water either this day or on the previous day.

Greg could not believe that his son had become so stubborn. He tried to make Matthew understand that if he had done something wrong, it was only making matters worse by continuing to lie.

Matthew responded that he was not lying.

Feeling as though he had failed, Greg thought it best to let the matter drop until a time when Matthew was not so upset.

With this unpleasant matter in the background, the family finally settled in for the night. Shortly after midnight, Sandy was suddenly awakened by the sounds of loud sobbing coming from somewhere in the house. Thinking it was one of the children, Sandy quickly roused her husband and together they made their way to the children's bedrooms. To their relief, but to their surprise, they found both Matthew and Rebecca sound asleep in their beds.

Surely, Sandy had not imagined or dreamed the sobbing. She must have been asleep.

As Greg and Sandy made their way back to their bedroom, they suddenly heard the sobbing again—slow, deep sobbing sounds, as if someone was in a deep state of sorrow. They searched the house but could not find the source of the sobbing. After about 15 minutes, the sobbing stopped and both Greg and Sandy were left wondering what was happening in their new home.

Although unnerved, the couple decided not to tell anyone about the incident. As the days slipped by, they tried to put it out of their memories, choosing not to discuss it among themselves.

A few weeks later, early in September, as Sandy went about cleaning the upstairs, she overheard voices coming from Rebecca's bedroom. Matthew was now in school so she knew Rebecca could not be speaking to him. She assumed her daughter was playing dolls and maybe having a pretend tea party or something similar. Just the same, she decided to check on her daughter.

Sticking her head in through Rebecca's bedroom door, she saw her daughter sitting on the bed conversing with someone. But there was no one else in the room.

"Who are you talking to, Rebecca?" Sandy asked.

"The lady," Rebecca quickly replied.

"What lady?"

"The lady who was here before you came in. She's gone now. She left when you opened the door."

Although Rebecca insisted that there had been a woman in her room that day, Sandy believed that her daughter must have an overactive imagination.

Several weeks later, however, she heard Rebecca having a similar conversation in the room.

"Are you talking to that lady again, Rebecca?" Sandy asked upon entering the room.

"No. I'm talking to 'Kyle' [a pseudonym]."

"Kyle? Who is Kyle, Rebecca?"

"He's a little boy who lives in the house and he plays with me a lot."

Choosing not to press her daughter on the matter, Sandy left the room. She was now becoming concerned over what was happening in her house. First the sobbing, now her daughter was talking to people who weren't there. By now, Sandy had forgotten about the wet footprint incidents.

As Rebecca's conversations continued, Sandy and Greg were at a loss over what to do. Perhaps their young daughter merely had an overactive imagination. What else could it be?

Greg may have inadvertently learned the answer to their questions during an innocent conversation over lunch at his office. He can't remember how he and his co-workers got onto the subject of ghosts, but he innocently commented to his colleagues that he sometimes wondered if his house wasn't haunted. He told his co-workers about the sobbing and his daughter's visitors. When one of his colleagues, a woman in her mid-fifties, said that she wasn't surprised to hear there might be ghosts in the house, he asked her to explain.

The woman told him that when she was a child she remembers a great tragedy that had befallen the family who lived in Greg's house at the time. As she recalled it, one August morning, the boy who lived there—who was eight or nine years of age—drowned in the ocean. She believed the drowned boy's name was "Kyle" (again, not his given name) and she also remembered that the mother was devastated and eventually the family had to move from the house to get her away from the place where her son had drowned.

It was like a light bulb had come on. It all fit.

Greg and Sandy now believe that, taken together, the sobbing, Rebecca's visitors and the wet footprints on the stairs (which still turn up every now and then) all add up to one thing—their house is haunted by the ghost of the drowned boy and his mother.

Moving Pictures

A few years back, a group of Nova Scotia lawyers may have received more than they bargained for when they purchased an old home in Dartmouth with plans to turn the structure into their firm's new law office.

Early in 2001, two metro-area law practices merged into one larger firm and looked for larger quarters. Eventually they were drawn to a home that had most recently been occupied by a pair of elderly women who are both now deceased. The house had a great deal of character and had just come on the market. However, Darrell Dexter, one of the partners in the new firm and an elected member of the Nova Scotia legislature, confirmed that almost immediately there were reports of strange things happening in the house.

For starters, he says, many people reported seeing an image of a person in one of the upstairs windows, only there was no one in the house at the time of the reports. As well, those in the house reported hearing strange, inexplicable noises. Furthermore, Darrell says they have proof that something unusual is connected to the house. When appraisers took photos of the structure, they knew for sure there was no one inside, yet in some of the photos taken of the rear windows, a faint but distinctive outline of a person can be seen.

"I always keep an open mind about these things," Darrell says. "You can definitely see something in the window. I have never been afraid of the dark or necessarily believed in ghosts, but you do reach a point where you begin to wonder if maybe there are things out there that defy explanation."

For Darrell, that point may have arrived one day shortly after his firm purchased the home. He had dropped by with his son Harris to check out the premises. "We had heard the stories that maybe the house was haunted or something like that, but I don't think we took them seriously. We looked around the place for a few minutes and when I stopped to talk to some of the other people there, Harris took the opportunity to go off exploring on his own."

As Darrell discussed business, Harris ventured to the second floor, poking around the rooms as most curious kids would. Darrell says he thinks Harris may have been gone 10 or 15 minutes before he came back downstairs. Harris brought with him a most unusual picture—a framed, black and white, 5 x 7 photograph of one of the sisters who used to reside in the house.

"I asked Harris where he found the picture," Darrell recalls. "He told me it had been hanging in the middle of the wall in one of the rooms upstairs."

Darrell found this somewhat peculiar. He understood that all the personal belongings from the previous owners had been removed before the house was sold. He also knew the rooms on the entire second floor had been stripped to prepare for renovations. Darrell immediately showed the picture to the man who had been taking care of the house since the lawyers had purchased the property.

"I told him about the picture and where Harris said he found it. I thought he had left it on the wall for some reason, but I felt it belonged to the family of the previous owners. I felt we should make sure it was returned to them."

While Darrell expected to hand the picture over without incident, he was surprised at the other man's reaction.

"He was surprised that Harris had found the picture," Darrell says. "He told me that he had been in that room [many] times and he was a hundred percent certain that there was no picture on that wall. He insisted that if that picture had been there, he would have found it. It just wasn't there."

Considering the house's reputation, the man's declaration gave Darrell reason to pause. "I said to him, 'You have got to be kidding.' But he was very serious. Of course, our curiosity was then piqued. We marched my son back upstairs and got him to show us exactly where he found [the picture]."

Harris indicated that he had found the picture hanging in the middle of the wall in one of the upstairs bedrooms, where anyone who'd been in the room before would have most certainly found it.

"It may seem like we over-reacted, but all of a sudden we all got a strange feeling from standing in the room. We just couldn't explain it, but my friend insisted that before Harris found the picture, it most certainly was not hanging on the wall—that he was sure of."

Darrell can't say he believes that ghosts do haunt the house, but he is certain that weird things have happened there. "Let's just say that I'm an avid disbeliever in such things. I'm just saying that it's weird…very weird."

Tuned In

Founded in 1759, Liverpool, Nova Scotia, has a rich and colourful history that includes shipbuilding and privateering. It is also where Yvette and Rick Henneberry say they encountered a ghost.

Rick grew up in Liverpool where today he runs a small barber business on the town's main street. He met Yvette in 1994 and in the summer of 1995 the happy couple moved into their first apartment, not far from where Rick now operates his business. At first, they say, there was nothing out of the ordinary with their cozy little apartment, which was the ground floor of a two-storey building. Because there was an upstairs apartment, Rick and Yvette were not surprised to hear noises coming from up there.

"It was a nice little place," they agree. "We liked it there very much."

The couple were comfortable there—for at least the first three weeks.

Yvette was the first to come across the ghost, Rick says, explaining that after they had settled down in their new apartment, he became concerned when she repeatedly asked him if he heard the music. "I had no idea what she was talking about. I couldn't hear anything, but I concluded that if she was hearing music, it must be coming from the upstairs apartment."

However, he adds, there was a catch. On most of the occasions when Yvette asked Rick if he heard the music, there was no one home at the other apartment. "The young guy worked a lot and he lived there alone and it seemed like he was out of town all the time. It seemed like he was never at home, but we thought maybe when he left the apartment he left the television or stereo turned on. But when we asked him, he said no, he always made sure these things were turned off."

Yvette is a music teacher in the local school system and conducts private piano lessons. She described the music she heard as more like a music box than a radio, television or stereo. "I mostly heard it at night. Sometimes it woke me up. It was a steady tune, like you'd hear in an old-fashioned music box. It was nice and mellow, but also kind of eerie. I can't say it frightened me at all. It just made me curious about where it could be coming from."

They both agree that Yvette heard the music two or three times, but Rick couldn't hear it. "It kind of bothered me that she could hear it and I couldn't. I knew it didn't seem to frighten her or anything, but I couldn't understand why she could hear it and I couldn't."

That would eventually change.

One night, Rick recalls, he was suddenly wakened from a deep sleep by the gentle, steady sounds of a music box. "At first, I thought it must be coming from the upstairs apartment. Maybe our neighbour had come home and was listening to some music."

He quickly concluded, though, that he was mistaken.

Since Yvette was sound asleep beside him, Rick says he knew she couldn't be responsible for the music, but he couldn't distinguish its origins. Gently sliding out of bed so as not to disturb Yvette, Rick made his way through the small apartment in an attempt to locate the source of the music. No matter where he went, he says, the music followed him.

"Yvette was right. It did sound like an old-fashioned music box and no matter where I went, the music was always there. The strange part about it was that the volume never changed, it remained steady," Rick explains.

Try as he might, Rick could never locate the music's origin, but he says after that night he heard it more frequently. "After I heard it the first time, it would wake me up two or three times a week."

Both Rick and Yvette now could hear the music, but they both agree that it didn't bother them. "We weren't frightened by it," Yvette says. "In a way, it was soothing, but it did bother us that we couldn't explain where it came from."

As the music's rate of occurrence continued to rise, both Rick and Yvette also began to hear voices, as if people were talking. They also heard footsteps, as if people were walking around in the overhead apartment. As they had with the music, they assumed the voices were coming from upstairs, but after checking to see if their neighbour was home, they usually discovered there was no one else in the building—no one except ghosts, they concluded.

"When we heard these voices, we couldn't make out what they were saying," Rick explains. "It was barely audible, but it was there nonetheless. We weren't scared by this, but we knew something was there."

If the music, voices and footsteps weren't enough to scare the Henneberrys, their next paranormal experience did give them reason to pause.

Like the other incidents, this phenomenon occurred at night and it happened to Yvette.

"I was lying in bed," she begins, "facing the wall and Rick had his arm around me. I was kind of half awake and half asleep when I heard the water running in the bathroom down the hall and then I heard footsteps coming up the hall toward the bedroom. I was scared, I'll admit that, because if Rick was in bed with me, I wondered who was in the bathroom and who was coming into the bedroom."

Yvette lay quietly in the bed as she heard the door swing open and heard the footsteps approach the bed. The footsteps then stopped at the foot of the bed.

"Okay, I was freaked. If Rick's here beside me with his arm around me, who's standing by the bed? I had no idea what I expected to see when I turned around, but I slowly turned my head fully expecting to see a ghost. That would be natural after what we had been experiencing in the house."

Instead, Yvette was spooked by what awaited her.

"As I turned my head, I was stunned to see Rick standing there at the foot of the bed. Someone else was in bed with me."

Rick continued the story: "I heard the music and got up to look for it. Then I got a glass of water before coming back to bed. I remember seeing her face when she turned around. It was a look of total shock and surprise."

Yvette says as soon as she realized Rick wasn't in bed with her, the form disappeared. "But it was there. It felt just like a human body lying up against me with its arm around me. If none of the other experiences bothered me, that one sure did."

In the fall of 1995, Rick and Yvette moved out of the apartment, but not because they were afraid. Yvette had taken another job in a nearby community and they had to move there. They both admit they had never given much thought to the possible existence of ghosts or other such paranormal activity before they lived in that apartment. Today, however, they are convinced that something was with them—something that defies any conventional explanation.

The Tie That Binds

Cape Breton Island, joined to mainland Nova Scotia by the Canso Causeway, is well-known for hospitality, great food, hard-working residents and an economy closely tied to the land and the sea. But Cape Breton is also known for its ghosts.

Tales of ghosts, phantoms and other supernatural occurrences have been handed down from one generation to the next. The villages and closely-knit communities that dot the island are filled with such stories. One of these stories comes from the small city of Sydney.

"Heather" tells a tale of a haunted house so bizarre it is almost unbelievable. Heather recalls her childhood visits to her grandparents' home in one of Sydney's quaint neighbourhoods. She loved to visit her grandparents. "They were very special people—very loving and generous and always willing to share stories of the old days. They always put us kids first. I loved them very much."

She believes it was that deep love for her grandfather that resulted in the strange phenomena that occurred in the house following his death.

"Granddad was 82 when he died. He had always been very healthy. I don't think I can recall him ever being sick. That's why it came as a shock when he died of a heart attack," Heather says. "It was a terrible time for the family, especially my grandmom. She loved the old man with all her heart. They had been together for almost 60 years and they went through a lot. When you've been with someone that long, it's hard to let go."

After her grandfather's death, Heather says her grandmother found it difficult to stay in the house by herself, so members of the family, including the grandchildren, took turns staying at the house with the elderly woman. Heather was 15 at the time and she willingly agreed to stay with her grandmother. "I loved her dearly. I'd do anything for her, but I have to admit, after the first night there, it became a hard thing to do."

Heather's turn to stay at the house came about three weeks after her grandfather's funeral. "Me and grandmom had a great time together. We played a little cards, watched some TV, but mostly we just talked about happier times when we were all together. She loved to talk about Granddad. She believed he was her soul mate, [that] they were meant to be together for all eternity."

That night, at bedtime, Heather kissed her grandmother on the cheek after walking her to her bedroom. Then she slipped into the next room down the hallway. She wanted to be close in case her grandmother called on her during the night. But Heather had a problem staying asleep, and after about three hours of sleep, she awoke and had a difficult time getting comfortable again.

"That's when it all began. Everything felt different," Heather says. "It's hard to put in words, but the room felt weird. I had never felt like that before in my grandparents' house. It made me uncomfortable."

Sitting up in the bed, Heather noticed the door to her bedroom was open. She thought that was strange because she was sure she had almost closed it, leaving it open only a crack so that she could hear her grandmother if the elderly woman called. "It was a habit. We always closed our bedroom doors. Granddad said keeping the doors closed kept the heat inside, something very important on a cold winter night."

But now the door was open. Heather slid out of bed, made her way to the door and glanced out to see if maybe her grandmother was up and about. She was not.

As she walked into the hallway, Heather was startled to find all the bedroom doors wide open and all the lights in the upstairs turned on—all except the light in her grandmother's room. Sneaking to that door, Heather looked inside, expecting find her grandmother awake. Instead, the elderly woman was sound asleep.

"I have to admit that at that point, I was afraid. There was no explanation for those lights being on…none whatsoever."

Slowly, as if expecting to find someone inside one of the rooms, Heather made her way from one bedroom to the next, turning off the lights as she went. "I guess it was stupid in a way. I don't know what I would have done if I had found someone there. It was only me and grandmom in the house. What could we have done against an intruder?"

After turning off all the upstairs lights, Heather says she was too nervous to sleep. It was now about two in the morning and she hoped maybe there was something good on the television. Making her way downstairs and into the kitchen, Heather was startled to find all the lights on. "It was the weirdest thing I had ever seen. I know we had turned those lights off before we went upstairs, but they were all on."

Just as she had done upstairs, Heather went room to room and turned off all the lights. "By now, I was scared to death. There was no way I was staying down there by myself. I went back to my room, jumped into bed and pulled the blankets up over my head. I was scared. I'll admit that."

The next day, Heather says, she told her grandmother about the lights and she was surprised at the elderly woman's response. "She said, 'Oh that. That's nothing to worry about.

Stuff like that's been happening a lot since your granddad passed on. He's just trying to tell me he's all right and that I shouldn't worry.' "

Heather says the family came to accept these strange phenomena as her grandfather's way of communicating with the woman he loved. Heather has heard stories of many unexplained events from other family members who stayed with her grandmother from time to time. "Of course, others had the experience with the lights, but some said they saw doors and windows open and close on their own. Others said they saw things move about, like pictures on the walls, that sort of thing. Only one person ever said they actually saw Granddad—that was my father's sister. She said one night she watched as Granddad came up the stairs and went into the bedroom he had shared for so many years with Grandmom. That's the only time that I can recall anyone saying they saw him."

As far as Heather knows, the strange occurrences at the house stopped after her grandmother died about two years later. "The house was sold and I've never heard of anything happening there. I think once she died, he was at rest because they were finally together again."

Does the bond of love transcend this material world and connect to that other mysterious world that lies beyond? Heather believes it does. "I think love is a strong connection. These two people were deeply in love. They respected each other and took care of each other. I think it was only natural that he would still want to care for her even after his own death. I like to think that even death couldn't keep these two special people apart."

If that's the case, then maybe love is the tie that binds.

Need a Hand?

Annapolis Royal was founded as Port Royal by the French explorer Sieur de Monts in 1605. The settlement was destroyed in 1613 by English colonists under the command of Samuel Argall but was later rebuilt by the French.

The fort changed hands between the French and the English five times between 1605 and 1710, when it capitulated to a force of New Englanders under Francis Nicholson. The name was then changed to honour Queen Anne. Annapolis Royal was the capital of Nova Scotia from 1713 to 1749. Fort Anne Historic National Park includes the ruins of the original fort. The officers' quarters, completed in 1798, have been restored as a museum.

With so much history to draw from, it's no wonder Annapolis Royal has a ghost story or two.

Historian and ghost story buff George Munroe says the small town is rife with tales of the supernatural and the paranormal. He ought to know. When George was completing his university degree, he did his thesis on one of the town's local stories.

"If you go to Annapolis Royal, you will find a branch of the Royal Bank in a brick building. It was built in the early part of the 20th century. On that location, before the bank was built, there was a huge storey-and-a-half colonial house that had belonged to Sir William Fenwick Williams. Some people believed that that Sir William was the bastard son of Prince Edward, the Duke of Kent, and it was said that Sir William was quite a character."

The man who was thought to be Sir William's father was the barracks master at Fort Anne. The young Sir William rose rapidly through the ranks of the British military to become a

In a house where this building now stands, a spectre was said to carry his severed left hand in his right.

general. He fought in the Crimean War and he was well-regarded as a soldier because he and his troops held off an attack by the Turks during the war. For his bravery and leadership, Sir William was greatly decorated, but he never returned to Nova Scotia.

However, George points out, Sir William is still an important character in this story, since it is in his house where the ghost eventually manifests itself. "While Sir William never returned to Nova Scotia, the house remained in the ownership of his parents for many years. After his mother and father died, the house went through a number of owners and those who lived there said it was haunted."

From time to time, the home's various occupants reported that an earthly wailing could be heard throughout the house and occasionally a figure wearing the uniform of a Royal Engineer Lieutenant could be seen wandering through the house.

"According to local folklore, the uniform was from the 1840s because it was blue with red facing," George continues.

"It is said a ghostly image of a man in that uniform would appear. In his right hand he would be holding his left hand that had been severed at the wrist. The spectre would appear and then vanish, and each time the man seemed to be in a great deal of pain, as one could imagine if your hand had been severed."

In 1900, the owners of the house decided to sell the property to the Royal Bank, or the Union Bank as it was known back then. To make way for the construction of the new brick building, the old Williams house was cut into two pieces. One piece was moved to one end of Annapolis Royal, while the second piece was moved to another location at the other end of town. As far as George knows, each section was turned into dwellings that are still used.

"However, the real catch in this story comes at the time of separation," George says. "When they started to excavate for the foundation of the new bank, they found the remains of an engineer lieutenant under one of the walls where the old house had been resting. Lo and behold, they discovered that while most of the skeletal remains were intact, the left hand was severed and was, indeed, being held by the right hand."

The remains were given a decent and proper burial in Annapolis and, according to local legend, the ghost was never heard or seen again.

But who was this ghost? Was it mere coincidence that the ghost's left hand was severed like the left hand of the skeletal remains uncovered on the site?

George doesn't think so.

In fact, he refers to old garrison documents that reveal a soldier had been reported missing by his fellow soldiers. He was never seen or heard from again, which George says may have been a common occurrence in the past. However, while he says he believes that the remains, the ghost and the missing engineer are all one and the same, there was never any explanation for his severed left hand or how he came to be buried under the house.

"It's a great mystery and it's one of my favourite ghost stories," George says. "And as with all good ghost stories, there doesn't appear to be any reasonable explanation."

Then again, he adds, that's what makes it a ghost story.

One of the Family

Saint John, New Brunswick, was discovered by Europeans in 1524, although Basque, Breton and Norman fishermen are believed to have made voyages to the Bay of Fundy in the early 1500s. The French explorers Sieur de Monts and Samuel de Champlain arrived at the mouth of what is now the Saint John River on June 24, 1604. This was the feast day of St. John the Baptist, and the explorers named the river in the saint's honour.

The settlement was occupied in 1758 by the British and renamed Fort Frederick. The fort was destroyed by American revolutionaries in 1775, but was replaced by Fort Howe. The settlement began to develop in 1783 when the United Empire Loyalists established Parr Town and Carleton around the harbour. In 1785, the two communities amalgamated as Saint John to become Canada's first incorporated city.

Thousands of Irish immigrants were quarantined on Partridge Island (a small island near Saint John) during the Great Famine in Ireland. Many died crossing the ocean in unsanitary cargo ships. Hundreds more who survived the journey died on the overcrowded island from inadequate shelter, medical care, sanitation and drinking water. Those hardy enough to make it ashore faced continued poverty and prejudice in the search for employment in the Loyalist city. An Irish community was established in Saint John during the late 19th century, but it diminished somewhat over the years, since immigrants who had the means to travel further abroad sought better opportunities in the west and south in the United States.

One Saint John woman says the Irish legacy continues to haunt the city. Although she chooses not to reveal her identity, she says she believes the ghosts of those who suffered and died on Partridge Island remain, still looking for food and relief from their misery. On clear moonlit nights, she says, it is possible to hear the moans and groans of those poor lost souls. And, she adds, if one is lucky, it is sometimes possible to see an image of one of those who died so long ago walking the streets near the waterfront.

Despite her deep belief in Saint John's Irish spirits, the woman's ghost story is more personal. "I live with a ghost," she says matter-of-factly. "I don't think it's one of the long-lost Irish, but someone who lived in this house long ago."

While she is not exactly sure how old her house is, she says records suggest it is well over 200 years old. "That's a lot of time for a house to be standing and that means there's a lot of history in those walls," the woman says. "I'm sure I've felt and experienced some of that history."

After moving into the stately home some 30 years ago, she says the ghost remained dormant for about five years before "all hell broke loose."

The first time she and her family encountered the ghost was on Christmas Eve, 1970. "We were all gathered in the large sitting room when one of my sons asked who was upstairs. I told him no one was upstairs because we were all down here next to the tree. He replied that a man was at the top of the stairs when he walked by on his way to join the rest of us. Well, I told him, he must be mistaken. There was no one upstairs. However, just to ease to his mind, my husband went up to check things out. He didn't find anything."

After that, our storyteller says, apparitions of the strange man regularly appeared throughout the house. Primarily, the man was seen at the top of the stairs. Once, she says, one of her daughters reported seeing a man in the basement, but she didn't stick around long enough to see who or what it was. "It could have been my daughter's imagination, but she insisted it was a man. Because of what we've seen in the house, I believe her."

"Mostly, when we see him, he's dressed in a soldier's uniform of some kind. It's usually quite dark, but he's dressed in blue and he appears to be sporting a sword on his side. Other than that, I'd say the gentleman is about six feet tall and you can never see his face so it's impossible to give a description."

The apparition can last for varying lengths of times, but mostly it becomes visible for a moment or two, then disappears. "One night, while I was lying in bed waiting for my husband to join me, I saw the soldier walk down the hallway, pause at the top of the stairs then turn to come into our bedroom. But he never made it. He just vanished. Another time, I saw him take the same route, only this time he went down the stairs. At first, these sightings used to frighten me, but not anymore. I think we're just used to it, but it has frightened many of our guests who have seen it."

Besides the sightings, she says, they have experienced other paranormal happenings in their home. "It's very common to find things moved from one location to another. When we came downstairs one morning, we found all the pictures on the walls of our living room turned around with the faces against the wall. Other times, the cupboard doors in the kitchen would open and close as if someone was looking for something. And sometimes we'd lose things and find them weeks later in a totally different location…things like toothbrushes and combs. They'd disappear from the bathroom and turn up sometimes in the kitchen or the basement or even outside. We can't explain it."

Despite these strange goings-on, the woman says she and her family take the happenings in stride. "We figure whoever it is thinks the home still belongs to him. Besides, if something was going to hurt us, I'm sure it would have hurt us already. We really don't feel threatened by the presence. We just consider him one of the family."

The Stranger Beside Me

People who encounter a ghost usually remember the experience for the rest of their lives. That's the case for Bridgewater, Nova Scotia, resident Audrey Doane, who remembers having a ghostly experience in 1958. At the time, Audrey was 13 and living with her family at Hawk Point on the very southern tip of Cape Sable Island, not too far from Yarmouth.

The haunted house was one that Audrey baby-sat at. The ominous three-storey house had 13 rooms. "The house had sat empty for many, many years. I remember my parents telling us kids that it was a haunted house and that a very old, grumpy man had lived there. They called him Bub."

By the time Audrey began baby-sitting at this particular house, the old man had been dead for many years, and, as Audrey explained, "the house had been closed up for a very long time until his granddaughter moved in with her family. She had three very small children, all under the age of six."

Although the idea of going to the purportedly haunted house didn't excite her, Audrey says that the chance to earn a few cents baby-sitting was worth the risk.

"Whenever I went there, the young mother always made sure the small children were in bed. I would arrive at about six thirty or thereabouts, then we'd go over the regular baby-sitting routine and other chores that I could do," Audrey recalls. "The house was always very quiet. There was no television so I'd read a lot and do my homework."

As well, Audrey says, the young family always appreciated when she did some household chores to help them out. "I always wanted to be busy, so it was natural for me to find work to do. Right off the kitchen there was another little room where the mother kept her ironing. I'm not really sure, but I think it would have been the old man's bedroom. One evening, I thought I'd help by doing some of the ironing. Since the children were sleeping, I pulled down the ironing board in that room and went to work. No sooner had I started when I felt this light tap, tap, tap on my shoulder. Quickly, I looked around but there was no one there. The children were all in bed and there was no one else in the house with me."

Repositioning the ironing board again so she could maintain a better view of the door, Audrey went to work again. Suddenly, she felt the tap, tap, tap on her shoulder once again.

"After it happened this time, I just left the room. I was very frightened. My hair was standing on ends."

When the parents came home, Audrey immediately left. She did not tell them of her experience. Some time later, however, she had another unexplained experience in the house.

"This time, it was in the afternoon when I was baby-sitting. The children were all downstairs with me. I knew there was no one else in the house other than me and the children, but I heard, several times, someone clomping up and down the stairs. I looked everywhere, but I couldn't find anyone. I was terrified and I was very glad when the parents returned home so I could get out of there."

Although Audrey was growing timid about returning to the house, she agreed to baby-sit on another occasion. It was the seven-to-nine shift. "I don't really know what possessed me to help with the chores again, but for some reason I thought I'd try ironing again. I went into the little room near the kitchen and got down to work. Within minutes, the tapping happened again. I moved around, but it did it again. I moved again, and it followed me again."

Each time, Audrey says, the tapping became more forceful. "I got the distinct feeling that whatever this was, it was telling me to get out of that room and not to come back. When I glanced around quickly one time, I thought I saw a shadow but I can't say for sure."

Understandably, the next time the young mother asked her to baby-sit, Audrey refused. "I wasn't going back there. It was clear that whatever was there didn't want me around."

The Fighting Ghosts

Valerie Evans of Saint John, New Brunswick, wonders if she is more susceptible to paranormal experiences than other people. In at least two homes she's lived in she's witnessed phenomena that defy logical explanation. Since they can't be easily explained, she concludes that she is more tuned in to that "other" world.

Valerie's first experience with the supernatural happened several years ago when she and her family lived in the south end of Saint John. Her daughter, Tracey, was 14 at the time, and Valerie says they experienced the presence together.

"We were living in a big old house. I'd guess it was probably built in or around 1880," Valerie begins. Before moving into the house, which included another apartment, she says they had never heard of anything unusual happening there. "When we began experiencing things, it came as a total shock to us. For starters, we had a dog and it would often stand and stare at this certain corner for the longest while. It would roll its head back and forth and whine as if it was listening to or watching something, but none of us ever saw anything."

For the most part, she explains, the phenomena seemed to be confined to the basement. "We were never able to keep warm in the house, mostly because we couldn't keep the basement door closed. No matter how many times we closed it and locked it, it would always come open. It was the weirdest thing. No matter what we did to close that door, it would always come open."

On one occasion, Valerie says, the man who lived in the other apartment decided he had had enough. "He put a hook on the door itself and put the eye on the door casing. He hooked it and said 'There, that should keep it shut.' Those old-fashioned hooks are pretty effective. We thought it would stay closed."

But to their surprise, it didn't work.

"A little while later, as I came around the house, I found the door was open again. I was shocked. There was no way it could have come open on its own, but there it was. This time, I hooked the lock myself and I twisted the eye so that the hook was pretty tight. When Tracey came along, I told her not to worry because this time I had fixed it so that it wouldn't come open."

All of a sudden, Valerie says, she and her daughter watched in amazement as the door began to shake violently as if someone was on the other side pushing it. "Then, as we stood there and watched, the hook came undone and the door flung open with such a force that we had to jump out of the way or it would have knocked us over. I said, 'Fine, if you like the door open, you can have the door open.' "

After that, Valerie says, they never bothered trying to close the basement door, and it did remain open. To this day, she can't explain what had happened at that house. "It was kind of spooky, but we never felt threatened in any way. It was just one of those strange things that you can never seem to explain."

That wouldn't be the only time Valerie would experience such strange things.

Some years later, Valerie and her family moved into a brand new townhouse on the opposite end of the city. "To my knowledge, nothing unusual had ever happened to anyone [in that townhouse] before we moved in."

But it didn't take long for Valerie to become aware of whatever strange force had been lurking in the house.

"On nights when my husband was working late, I would stay up watching television, waiting for him to come home. And every night, at exactly the same time, without fail, I would hear footsteps coming down the stairs. Then ever so lightly they'd go to the front door and very softly the door would open. When I'd go to look to see if someone was there, I never ever found anyone."

Although Valerie says she told her husband about the experiences, he dismissed her story. "He never believed me because he was never home to hear it for himself."

Eventually, though, that would change.

"One night, a friend was over and I knew it was getting close to the time when I would usually hear the footsteps. So I said, 'Listen,' and sure enough we could hear the footsteps come down the stairs and the door open. Our friend suggested that one of the children had been up, but then he realized there was no one there."

Some time later, Valerie says her husband finally became a believer.

"I had gone to bed but my husband was downstairs. All of a sudden he came flying into the bedroom. He said, 'I thought you told me that it was a friendly ghost.' I said, 'Yeah, it is.' He said, 'Oh no it isn't.' I was shocked. I had never experienced anything that would make me think otherwise."

Valerie's husband told her that he had been sitting in the living room when all of a sudden he heard an awful racket coming from the basement. "He had no idea what it was, but he went down to check it out. Once he got down to the basement, the noise stopped. Then all of a sudden he heard the noise again, only this time it had moved to the main floor, so he came back up to see if he could find its origin. When he got there, he found that the temperature had dropped a lot and it had grown very cold. As the noise escalated, he decided he wasn't staying there and that's when he came upstairs."

Valerie says they had no idea what her husband had just heard, "but whatever it was it had frightened him pretty badly. As we kept listening, we could actually hear something coming up the stairs. It sounded like two people were having a fight and were hitting each other. It was like they were throwing each other against the wall and it sounded pretty bad. Anyway, we listened as the noise came up the stairs. We could hear them coming closer and closer. As they got closer, the temperature in the bedroom dropped dramatically. It was really, really cold and it was scary. We had no idea what was going to happen but we did feel threatened by the noise. If it had come into the bedroom, I don't know what we would have done. Then, all of a sudden, it just stopped."

Later, Valerie and her husband learned that, according to one story many years earlier, there had supposedly been a murder committed on the same property where their house were built. It was suggested that the soft footsteps they heard were the woman tip-toeing out into the night to meet her lover, while the fighting sounds may have been from the altercation that left her lover dead.

Whatever the case, Valerie says they really don't have any other explanation about what they had experienced.

2
Haunted Places

Things That Go Thump in the Night

In the southwest corner of New Brunswick, about halfway between the New Brunswick-Maine border and the city of Saint John, is the small fishing village of Black's Harbour. Home to about 1000 residents, it is also the site of the Connors Brothers' Sardine plant, one of the largest sardine plants in the world.

Roger Mahar grew up in Black's Harbour and he's proud of his roots. As a local history buff, Roger knows a few of the area's local ghost stories. The one he particularly favours has origins that go back to the mid-1930s.

"The story goes that this German guy in his early forties showed up in town one day and decided to stay here. He had been in the First World War and had lost both of his legs. In their place, he had two wooden legs. He found a job at one of the steam plants at the sardine factory as an engineer and he ran the boilers on the night shift."

Roger continues, "It is said that the man was married to a pretty young woman and he found out that his wife was having an affair with the able-bodied younger man who he worked with on the night shift. This younger man was assigned to bring in the coal and to assist with the running of the equipment."

Predictably, Roger says, the man was devastated that he would be betrayed by his wife. "But somehow he found a way to forgive her and somehow they resolved to mend their differences and try to put this ugly affair behind them—or so he thought. One night in early February he found out differently."

Learning that his wife had continued to betray him was too much for the older man. "The two men were working down at the steam plant on this cold, blustery night in February. They had all the boilers stoked up good and full. The wind was blowing strong and hard and the snow was coming down heavy. Suddenly, one of the valves seemed to malfunction. The older man told his young colleague that he had to go to the boilers to fix the defective valve. The younger man insisted that he should go, but over the protests, the older man went. After about five minutes, the young fellow hears 'thump, thump.' "

Not knowing what the noise could have been, the younger man ran to the boilers. There he found the older man hanging from the pipes; he had committed suicide by kicking his wooden legs out from under himself.

"He tied a rope around his neck, threw it up over the pipe that connected to the boilers. There wasn't enough room between the boilers and the roof to hang himself, so he kicked his legs off."

But Roger says the story doesn't end there. "Right up until they tore the old steam plant down in 1997, people said every night in February when it was cold and blustery outside, you could hear two very distinctive thumps."

It's true, he insists. "No one ever saw anything, but lots of people said they heard the noise."

So there you have it. Proof that you should always be wary of things that go thump in the night, especially in February.

The University Ghost

Dalhousie University in Halifax, Nova Scotia, is recognized as one of the finest universities in Canada. With a student population of about 12,500, Dalhousie is one of the country's leading teaching and research universities.

Glenn Coolen, who founded Halifax Ghost Walks in 1990, says he had heard stories of a ghost at one of the Dalhousie residences for many years. In fact, he continues to hear new stories about the ghost even to this day.

"The ghost is said to haunt one of the women's residences, which was actually an older home converted into a residence for the university," Glenn explains. "Anyway, the most recent story I've heard about the residence involves a first-year student who was away from home on her own for the very first time. Now this young lady had brought with her many of the things that she felt would make her new dorm room more comfortable and homey. One of these was a collection of Russian stacking dolls."

Glenn says the first incident supposedly occurred only a few short weeks after the young lady moved in.

"She had placed her stacking dolls on a shelf at the other side of the room so that when she looked over, she would see something familiar," he says. "One morning after a restless sleep, when the girl woke up and looked over at the shelf, she saw that while the dolls were still lined up as she had placed them, they were now turned around and facing the opposite direction. But she hadn't turned the dolls and she was certain no one else had been in the room since she had the only key."

Although she couldn't explain the occurrence, she turned the dolls back in their original direction and went about her business. Soon she had forgotten about the dolls—until a few days later.

"Another morning, a few days after the dolls had been turned the first time, this young lady awoke again to see the dolls facing one more time in the opposite direction," Glenn says. "This time, she became quite upset. She checked the door and the windows and they were all locked. *How could the dolls be turned?* she wondered."

There was no obvious explanation, but that is not what finally drove her from the room.

Some time later, the girl had another paranormal experience in her residence, and this time she refused to stay. "One evening, as she was getting ready to go out, she turned off her blow dryer and put it down. But it kept on going. She made a mental note to have the blow dryer checked as she feared there must be an electrical short in the switch or wire. A night or two later, the same thing happened again, only this time when the girl pulled the plug the blow dryer kept on going."

It was more than she could take. She moved out the next day.

The Girl in the Old Town Clock

Among the many landmarks of historic Halifax, none is more recognizable than the Old Town Clock. According to information from Parks Canada, Prince Edward, the Duke of Kent, arranged for the turret clock to be manufactured for the Halifax garrison before his return to England in 1800. To house the clock a three-tiered, irregular octagon tower atop a building of classical Palladian proportions was erected on the glacis bordering Barrack Street (now Brunswick Street). The Town Clock officially began keeping time for the garrison on October 20, 1803, and has served the residents of Halifax ever since.

Today, the Town Clock is maintained and operated by Parks Canada. Although the caretaker position was eliminated in 1965, Parks Canada staff wind the clock twice a week to minimize stress on the mechanism. A major restoration project in 1990 returned the exterior facade of the building to its original Georgian elegance. The Town Clock is a rare and treasured cultural resource. It is a prominent symbol of Halifax's rich historical past and, according to some historians and storytellers, it is also haunted.

Although few modern-day sightings have been recorded, some claim that in the late 1700s, before the clock was built on its prominent location high atop the hill, a young girl fell into a deep well used to supply the garrison at the fortress. There, they say, she drowned in a deep watery grave. Her body was never recovered.

Some time after the clock was built, soldiers and others who entered the clock tower claimed they heard unusual

A girl who drowned in a well is said to haunt Halifax's Old Town Clock.

sounds throughout the structure, similar to a young girl crying and laughing. Other witnesses reported seeing ghostly images of a young girl moving throughout the clock tower. Today, the Town Clock remains locked to protect it for future generations. If the structure is haunted, the mystery remains hidden away behind closed doors.

The Ghost of Windsor House

The stately Windsor House Inn on Water Street in St. Andrews, New Brunswick, is one of the finest examples of a Georgian home in the Maritimes. Built in 1798 as the home of Captain David Mowatt and his wife Mehetible Caleff Mowatt, the newly renovated inn allows visitors to step back in time and experience the elegance of classic 19th-century comfort. It may also provide them with the opportunity to experience a ghost firsthand.

Jay Remer, who owns and operates the inn with business partner Greg Cohane, says that when they began renovating the structure in 1998, they could see the potential within the historic house. Though the renovation required a lot of hard work, they have been able to restore the home to its former magnificence, complete with museum-quality period furnishings and art. Over dozens of layers of old flooring and wallpaper, the pair have created a homey atmosphere with fine furnishings and a relaxed feel. As much of the original structure as possible has been preserved or painstakingly replaced with attention to authenticity.

The one thing they couldn't control, however, was the presence that still haunts the rooms of Windsor House. But Jay says they have no problem with it. If anything, the ghost adds character to the house and they know she means no harm. He refers to the ghost as "she" because they believe the ghost is the spirit of Mehetible.

To know the ghost, he says, one must get to know Mehetible. She was the eighth of eleven living children (four others had been stillborn) of Dr. John Caleff and his second wife, Dorothy Jewett. According to the book *Lady With a Past: The Restoration of a Georgian Home*, by Pamela Stuart,

Mehetible was a woman of great physical and moral strength. She was also a strong pillar of the small seaside community near the Maine-New Brunswick border.

Like many women of her day, Mehetible was destined to spend most of her energy bearing and raising children. When her husband, Captain David Mowatt, died at sea on August 21, 1810, Mehetible became solely responsible for raising her ten children, including a six-month-old daughter. Two years later, in October 1812, Mehetible's father died. In his will, Dr. Caleff recognized her spirit and generosity by leaving all his possessions to "that mirror of love and patience, my daughter Mehetible." After a long and eventful life, Mehetible died in 1860, at age 92.

During her life, Mehetible was a generous and respected citizen of St. Andrews. Jay believes that's why she still hangs around the house. While the ghost of Mehetible is mischievous and playful, she has not posed great problems for the home's owners, except for one incident in the fall of 1998. At the height of renovations, a valve broke in a second-floor bathroom, allowing 2000 gallons of water to spill into the rooms below.

"This was about two weeks before we were going to be hosting a special luncheon for the Lieutenant Governor of New Brunswick. We had gone to Ireland for a much-needed break before we opened. While we were gone, the valve broke. We had a lot of damage and lost a lot of time. It was then that we, jokingly at first, started saying that it must have been a ghost."

Today, Jay says he believes that was a prophetic statement because they now believe a ghost does, indeed, inhabit their inn.

One room in particular, which they believe was Mehetible's room, has been the epicentre for many strange phenomena. "We've had guests report all sorts of things happening in there. The door has slammed shut and the door has often locked by itself to the point that you can't get in or out. Other times, we've had the room fill with smoke, only there has been no fire. No one has actually seen the ghost, but they've felt her presence and they've seen pictures move. It's only in that one room and we figure it's Mehetible. She was a very formidable force in St. Andrews when she was alive and maybe she's not ready to go. Actually, we think she's protecting the house and really wants to make sure we are successful. She's quite friendly."

Despite tales of the ghost of Windsor House, the inn and the room are very popular with visitors. Jay says, "We've actually had people come specifically to stay in the room. It is very popular and we are convinced there is something special about the room. Some visitors, who had no way of knowing anything about the room, have also reported things. There's no proof that there's something in the room, but we're convinced there is. I feel very comfortable in there. You can feel her all around the room. It's just a special place."

The Ghost at the Privateer Inn

It was Christmas Eve, 1989. Susan Lane, manager of the historic Lane's Privateer Inn in Liverpool, Nova Scotia, was returning to the inn from her parents' house. The inn was closed for Christmas, so Susan had left it empty and believed it would be empty when she got back.

"As I was walking back over the bridge at about eleven o'clock, I looked up and I could see the blue flicker of a television in one of the windows on the third floor. Now I knew there was no one at the inn, I was absolutely certain of that. The place was closed up tight so I thought that was strange. I wondered if we had missed the television when we did a room check."

When she got to the inn, Susan went to the third floor. "When I got there, all the doors were open. Now normally those doors would all be closed and locked. And I knew they had been closed when we locked up for Christmas. It was unsettling, to be sure, but I still made my way down the hallway to room 134 where I thought the television was on. When I got there, I found that the television was on and the noise was blaring quite loud."

Inside the room, she says, it was very, very cold. She remembers that it was so cold she could see her breath.

"Not really understanding what was happening, I went in and turned off the TV. As I turned it off, the door to that room slammed shut and then I could hear all the other doors slamming closed one after the other, as if someone was running down the hallway closing them as they went. When I went to open the room's door to leave, it was locked."

Susan returned to the hallway and quickly made her way down the corridor, stopping at every room door along the way. They were all locked.

Lane's Privateer Inn in Liverpool, Nova Scotia, is the site of many unexplained phenomena.

"I don't know how that could have been. In those days, before we renovated, you had to manually lock those doors. It was impossible for them to lock and unlock themselves. There's just no way."

Susan isn't sure what happened at the inn that night but said it does appear that something besides the guests and employees inhabit the premises. "As far as I know there is nothing special or unique about room 134, only that it was in the old section."

Lane's Privateer Inn is at the mouth of the gently flowing Mersey River in Liverpool. The building was once the home of Captain Joseph Barss, Jr., one of the most famous privateers in the annals of Canadian history and certainly one of the most colourful characters in the history of Nova Scotia.

Ownership of the Barss property has changed hands many times, and the structure itself has undergone numerous renovations and additions. In 1947, a Liverpool couple, Helen and Edgar Lane, acquired the property and operated a variety of businesses at the location, including a furniture store, apartments, a bookstore and a jewellery store. In 1962, when the Lanes decided to turn the premises into an inn and dining room, their son Ron, who was finishing up a career in the air force, agreed to return to Liverpool to help out. Today, the Barss property continues to function as an inn, but it is now under the management of a third-generation Lane, as Ron's daughter Susan joined the family business in 1986.

Over the years, there have been many stories of the alleged haunting of Lane's Privateer Inn and the Barss property. While Susan points out that she has never heard stories that involve the old sea captain himself, she says "there are many legends and stories" that surround the historical structure.

"We've heard many of them over the years. Everybody who works here reports that they've encountered one thing or another…one of the most common reports is that people have seen someone come in the front door and then they're gone. Witnesses most often see a man in black and sometimes the bartenders will look up and see someone at the end of the bar, but there's really no one there. Sometimes all the bar stools are pushed back from the bar with no logical explanation. Some people have also said they've heard their names spoken when no one is around. Generally, most of the reports indicate it's a man, but I've experienced things that are connected to a female."

Susan says most of the reported phenomena happen at night. Her own personal experiences occurred not only at night but on Christmas Eve, although she notes that she does not believe that date has any significance for the property. "I'm not sure there's any other reason for that, except that Christmas is the only day of the year that we don't have guests and the dining room is closed so it's quiet and you can hear things that you wouldn't necessarily hear during a busy day."

Susan's first ghostly experience was on Christmas Eve in 1986. The place was very still and quiet, she recalls. "It was still relatively early and I had just returned from having dinner at my parents' home (at the other end of Liverpool). I was working in the office trying to get caught up on some paperwork when I heard it. The experience was very disturbing, but not frightening."

As Susan busied herself with her work, she says she began to hear someone crying. "Actually, I could hear a woman crying, like she was sobbing quietly. I looked all over the place and couldn't find a thing. There was nobody in the inn except for me. I'm sure of that, but that doesn't explain where the noise was coming from."

The thing that alarmed her the most, Susan says, is that no matter where she went in the large, rambling estate, the level of the sobbing remained constant. "Then, almost as quickly as I heard the sobbing, it stopped and almost immediately I began to hear a woman singing a lullaby. I'm sure it was a lullaby although I couldn't recognize the words. It was soothing and mellow and she kept repeating the song over and over as if she was trying to comfort someone, maybe a young child."

Susan says she believed the singing was coming from the second floor, so she made her way there, not really knowing what to expect. An inspection of the second floor didn't reveal the origin of the sound. "I looked everywhere, but I just couldn't find it. It would start and stop again. That went on for about half an hour. I wasn't at all frightened by this, but it was somewhat unsettling and even sad. I got the feeling this lady was very upset over something."

After that night, Susan says she continued to hear reports of ghostly sightings at the inn, and in light of her own personal experiences, she learned to accept what she heard. "Some staff members would tell us that they smelled a perfume, something like what their grandmother would wear, something very floral. They said they mostly noticed it in the bar area. Others said they saw things move and that pictures were out of place. It all became part of the inn's character."

Susan's father Ron says that over the years they had heard reports from guests and staff of strange things happening in room 134. "We've had reports of the doors opening and closing by themselves and of things moving about the room. We've also had guests tell us that they sensed a presence in that room and that the presence seems very distressed and uncomfortable. After Susan's experience, I began to pay closer attention to those reports."

Ron admits it may be coincidence, but many of the reports about strange happenings on the inn's third floor come from that room.

There may be a good reason for that.

Ron recalls hearing a story from many years ago when Liverpool was first being settled. It's said that a woman stole a loaf of bread to feed her children. Justice was harsh in those days and, as the story goes, the woman was hanged from a tree on the spot where Lane's Privateer Inn now sits.

Coincidence? Maybe, but so far no one has been able to explain the strange phenomena there.

The Haunting of St. Clemens

The idea of living in an old church converted into a home held great promise for Gerry Oram, an electrical engineer by trade and an artist by design. Gerry, who has worked for both the RCMP and the Department of National Defence, describes himself as a practical and curious man who never takes anything at face value. No matter what the mystery, he says, he must always try to find a logical explanation.

However, he quickly acknowledges that some things defy such an explanation. Such is the case with the property he purchased in 1992, an old church on the north side of Saint John, New Brunswick.

Gerry decided to purchase the former church because it would provide ample room to pursue his artistic career. It also had a certain personality he found intriguing. The structure, which he estimates is about 100 years old, housed an Anglican congregation until 1972. The same year, a woman—also an artist—bought the building and converted it into a home where she remained with her children until Gerry bought it from her. She sold it because her children had grown up and moved away and the house was simply too large for her needs.

"I didn't think anything about the house, or 'chouse' as I call it, when I bought it," Gerry says. "Everything seemed to be in order. I thought it would be a great place to work."

Furthermore, since the previous owner had never mentioned anything unusual about the property, he had little reason to worry.

"I bought the place, unpacked and moved in," he continues. "It was great and things were normal for several days until one night when I was sitting at my computer doing

A former Anglican church in Saint John is haunted by spirits of deceased parishioners.

some work. Just over my left shoulder I caught a glimpse of an older lady standing right beside me. I didn't turn around, but instead I quickly sketched what I was seeing. The woman wore a dark hat and had curly hair. She wore glasses and had on a black smock-type garment over a grey dress. She also wore black socks."

The lady remained by his side for several minutes, Gerry says, but when he finished his sketch and turned around, she was gone. "It was the weirdest thing. She was there one minute and then she was gone."

The incident puzzled Gerry, but as he says, "I really didn't think that much about it until I showed the sketch to a friend of mine who is an elder in the United Church. When I told him about what I had seen and showed him the drawing, he told me that I had described an old Anglican nun."

On another occasion, Gerry recalls that he had fallen asleep on a couch in the living room area. At three o'clock, he says he woke with a start and sat straight up. "From there, I looked over to where the front door is located in the vestibule. There, suspended in mid-air, was a little girl with her arms crossed and her legs folded. She had on a little white hat that kind of resembled a lampshade and she wore white stockings and black patent leather shoes."

Realizing he was seeing a ghost, Gerry says he recalled the words his father used to tell him. "He'd say, if you ever see a ghost you should ask it if there is anything you can do to help it."

So that's what he did.

"Is there anything I can do for you?" Gerry asked the little girl.

"Yes," she responded. "You can go to my grave."

"What?" Gerry asked. "What do you want me to do when I go to your grave?"

"You'll know what to do when you get there."

"What's your name?" Gerry asked.

"Marie."

"Marie what?"

"Marie Wilson," the girl answered.

"How old are you, Marie?"

"I am eight years old," she said as she vanished.

Unlike some of his previous experiences in the house, Gerry says the encounter with the little girl left him unnerved. It seemed to him that she was reaching out to him from the grave to ask him to help her with something, but he didn't know what.

"The next day, I started calling cemeteries around Saint John, asking if they had a grave for a Marie Wilson. Finally, after several calls, I learned that one of the Catholic cemeteries did have a grave for a Marie Wilson and I thought I had unlocked a mystery."

Only, Gerry adds, when he went to the grave in the Catholic cemetery, the mystery grew deeper.

"They did have a grave for a Marie Wilson, but according to the date on the marker, the woman there would have been 25 years of age when she died and it was a Catholic cemetery. I had seen the girl in an Anglican church and the girl was much younger."

Could this have been the same Marie Wilson who had contacted Gerry that night? He says he has never found the answer to that question.

It was not the last paranormal event in the house.

"On another occasion, I had two friends from New York come to visit for a few days. They had come up for a fishing trip, and while they thought they should stay in a motel, I insisted that they stay with me. On the first night, they spread their sleeping bags on the floor and went to sleep. I never told them anything about the strange things that happen around here."

The next morning, Gerry says, one of his friends was very upset.

"I asked him what was wrong. Didn't he sleep well? He told me that he had had a strange experience. He said at around three o'clock something woke him up. He said he was lying on his back and when he opened his eyes he looked right into the face of a young man who was bent over staring down at him. My friend's description of the young man, right down to the tweed hat and pantaloons that young men wore many years ago, was too detailed for it to have been a dream. He was shaken up pretty bad, so I told him about the things that happen around here. I also told him that the spot where he had put his sleeping bag is also the exact spot where the congregation used to place the coffin when they had a funeral—right under the chandelier."

Coincidence? Gerry doesn't know, but he is certain that the house's former identity as a church explains the many paranormal experiences that have occurred there. He has not been frightened by the events. "I never feel threatened. They really are benevolent ghosts. I've had hundreds of experiences. There are times when I'll sit right up in the middle of the night and I'll smell pipe tobacco as if someone had just blown it in my face. Sometimes when I'm walking about, I'll pass through a pillar of cold air and I'll smell lemon. They say that at one time women used lemon juice for perfume. There are times when I'll hear knocking on the walls and I'll often see an old man, bent over, walking down the hallway. There's also an old lady looking down at me from what used to be the loft."

Eventually, Gerry says, he decided to do some research to see if there was an explanation for what was happening at the house. He first contacted the previous owner and she confirmed that while she and her family lived there, they had many unusual experiences.

Next, Gerry looked into the church's history. He learned that the church was once known as St. Clemens Church and it had handled the overflow from St. Luke's Church in Saint John.

Investigating further, Gerry says he was surprised to learn that the previous owner was an artist. "I am also an artist. Does that have something to do with what happens at my house?"

That's a good question, Gerry says, but no one has yet to provide an answer.

The Mystery of Mahogany Manor

When guests of Saint John's stately Mahogany Manor started complimenting the proprietors for employing a nice old lady who tucked them in at night, the owners knew something strange was going on.

There *was* no old lady on staff.

Mahogany Manor, at 220 Germain Street, was built between 1902 and 1905 by William Cross, a Saint John businessman who was a deacon in the Germain Street Baptist Church next door. The house is a combination of Queen Anne and Craftsman architectural styles. The homes on the tree-lined residential street in "uptown" Saint John feature fine woodwork, spacious rooms, ornate carvings and stained glass. Mahogany Manor has spacious living areas and five guest rooms, all lovingly restored to the classic elegance of the turn of the 20th century. Careful attention has been paid to the quality and craftsmanship of the original appointments—details that unwittingly led to the manor's haunting by a former occupant.

The present owners, Carl Trickey and Jim Crooks, purchased the property in August 2001. They report that the house's history makes for some interesting discussions, especially during tours of the home.

"We always take guests to the Cranberry Wine Room," Carl says, pointing out that some of the features there play a prominent role in the mystery of Mahogany Manor. "In that room, the headboard on the bed was made from the original front door of the house. It was made of mahogany and was very beautiful. The headboard still has the mail slot in it.

Similarly, hanging in the front window of the house is the original glass from the entrance."

As Carl points out, there's a reason for that.

To understand the reason, he adds, it's important to look back many decades in the home's history.

"There was a Mrs. McLean who used to live here long before the house became a bed and breakfast. The McLeans were a prominent family back then and they played an important part in the city's social and economic life. They owned the house for three or four decades and had it turned into apartments in the 1940s. Mrs. McLean lived in one of those apartments on the first floor."

Carl explains: "Mrs. McLean apparently died here. And for many years after she died, other residents of the house would claim that they had seen Mrs. McLean wandering through the hallways wearing the long white nightdress she was known to have worn in the last few years of her life."

In 1990, the previous owners decided to turn the premises into a bed and breakfast—an effort that would require substantial renovations and construction.

"They had heard the stories of the ghost of Mrs. McLean but they don't ever recall seeing her for themselves, except one time when one of the owners was working in one of the back bedrooms and he saw a blur of white pass by the door. At first he thought it must have been his partner, but when he went to check he found his partner was still sound asleep. Perhaps half jokingly, he concluded that he must have just seen the ghost of the old lady."

In 1994, when renovations were under way, the owners decided to remove the front door and put in a smaller one, since the original was very heavy and awkward for people to use. That's when the next set of sightings began.

"After they opened for business as a bed and breakfast, this friendly old woman would appear to guests…The guests were quite certain that she was a real person who would always appear around eleven o'clock at night. She would appear and would be very friendly and nice. She would tuck the guests in and make them feel at home," Carl says. "The next morning, the guests would come down and comment that the old lady was such a sweet person. The guests said it was so nice to have her come to see them in the evening. It made everyone feel so good about being here."

These reports recurred regularly, with the woman appearing mostly to single females and male-female couples.

"This went on for some time," Carl says, "until one time a clairvoyant, who was attending a psychic fair in the city, came to stay at the house. Just a few moments after she arrived she told the owners that they had a spirit in their house that was very upset by something that they had done." Of course, the owners wanted to know what they'd done to upset the spirit, and the psychic told them that she'd need some time to sort things out. As Carl explains, "Over the next day or so, this clairvoyant heard that the spirit was upset because she used to have the freedom of moving in and out of the home. Now she couldn't do that anymore because they had changed something in the house."

The owners told the clairvoyant that they had changed the front entrance of the house. The psychic suggested that the renovation was the problem.

"She told them that a spirit will usually pass through crystal or glass of some sort. By changing the door, they had prevented this spirit from being able to do what she'd done for so many years. She was making herself known to people in an effort to resolve this problem."

The clairvoyant suggested that the proprietors hang a crystal in the front entrance. "So in one of the flat glass windows in the new entrance they placed a teardrop crystal, and the spirit was not seen by guests for months and months," explains Carl.

Then one day, guests reported seeing an elderly woman in white in their rooms who was very nice.

The proprietors wondered how that could be if the crystal was still hanging in the window. But when they investigated, they found that the crystal was no longer there. The string had broken and the crystal was found in a shoe that had been near the doorway directly under the window.

"So they not only put the crystal back up again, but they also brought up the original piece of glass that had been in storage in the basement and hung it in the front window. As far as we know, the spirit has not been seen since."

Although his children and some of the guests have suggested removing the crystal to see what would happen, Carl says both the crystal and the original glass continue to hang in the entrance.

3

Public
Hauntings

The Girl in the Pasture

Milton, Nova Scotia, is nestled along the banks of the gently flowing Mersey River outside Liverpool. It was once called The Falls and was home to several sawmills. Today, its natural beauty is its main asset, and visitors from near and far travel to the picturesque village.

Milton is a safe and peaceful community in which to raise a family and put down roots. Ralph Rafuse has lived in Milton all his life and married a local girl, Annabel Veinot. After he returned from the Second World War, he and Annabel settled down in Milton to raise a family. Today, he still enjoys sharing stories of his childhood and memories of life in earlier times.

Occasionally, he will also share a ghost story. "Many years ago," Ralph begins, "when I was just a young fellow, I saw a ghost in Cowie's pasture, just as sure as I'm sitting here."

Cowie's pasture was a small field between Liverpool and Milton. Today, alders and bushes have grown over it. Years ago, however, Ralph recalls that many of the local farmers kept their cattle there.

"I was walking home [to Milton] this one night. It was before the war, I know that much. As I got close to Cowie's pasture, I could see a girl there all dressed in white. At first I thought it was one of the girls who lived near our home, but as I went up to speak to her, she just disappeared. Just like that," Ralph says with a snap of his fingers. "She was gone. She didn't say a word."

Strangely enough, Ralph says, he could never figure out who the girl was. "I could see her just as plain as day even

Ralph Rafuse saw an apparition of a girl in this pasture near Milton, Nova Scotia.

though it was at night. I could see she had long hair, but I couldn't see her face. People always said the pasture was haunted. Now I know it to be true."

The Pirate of Grand Manan

Grand Manan is a small collection of communities in southern New Brunswick, not far from the U.S. border. About 3000 people live and work in seaside communities whose names reflect the geography. These names include North Head, Grand Harbour, Seal Cove, Seal Island and Southern Head. Grand Manan is so close to the border that Seal Island was once considered part of the United States.

According to Grand Manan resident Vern Bagley, a ghost pirate haunts the waters near Long Pond, Big Pond and the Anchorage Bird Sanctuary. About 15 or 20 years ago, he came face to face with the pirate. "And to tell you the truth," Vern says, "I don't ever want to do that again."

Vern admits the encounter left him shaken. "He scared me. Let's be up front about that…he scared me half to death and I never want to see him again. There was definitely something about his face that was very frightening. I can't describe it, but it wasn't good."

Recalling the incident, Vern says it was early morning and everything indicated that it was going to be a nice day. Armed with his binoculars, Vern was patrolling the waterways of the Anchorage Bird Sanctuary. He took his responsibilities very seriously. "Someone has to look out for the birds and ducks," he replies, noting that special places such as bird sanctuaries be preserved. He is very committed to the protection of his feathered friends.

"So there I was that day," Vern continues, "just looking around the area with my binoculars. There wasn't anything strange about the day, not that I could tell. But by and by, I noticed this guy coming towards me. I remember thinking to myself, *Who in the heck could that be at this hour?* I didn't really think there was anyone out there that morning except for me so I was curious to find out who was coming toward me."

The closer the figure got, however, the more nervous Vern became. "I could begin to see him very clearly. He was big…very big. And he was dressed like a pirate that you might see in them pictures from the olden days a long time ago. I really didn't know what to do. So I just stood there, expecting him to say something to me."

As Vern watched in amazement, the pirate came closer and closer until "he was right next to me. The closer he got, the funnier I felt. It wasn't natural, I'll tell you that much. I knew this guy wasn't supposed to be there. *Who in the heck dresses like that these days?* I thought to myself. I knew from his clothes that this wasn't normal."

Vern remained still and quiet as the mysterious figure stopped and looked directly at him with such intensity that he felt cold chills up his spine. "I didn't know what was going to happen next. Then, all of a sudden, he just let out one God-awful growl…Yup, he roared at me. It was like nothing I'd ever heard before. He didn't say anything, just roared. I was scared. I didn't know what the heck was going on, but I knew in my heart I didn't like him."

Then, Vern says, almost as quickly as the figure appeared, he turned as if to walk away, "but all of a sudden he just disappeared. Just like that," Vern says, snapping his fingers for emphasis. "He was gone—and I was glad. I didn't hang around after that. I got out of there pretty darn quick."

In the years following the sighting, Vern tried to find clues to the mysterious pirate's identity, but he has never been able to uncover anything. "I know for sure that I never, ever want to see him again. There was something about his face that really scared me and I think the next time I'd run away—fast."

The Phantom Fisherman

Shirley Chesley lives in a small community in New Brunswick known as Pocologan. She is fully versed in the folklore and graciously relates one tale she has heard over the years concerning ghosts at nearby Chance Harbour, where local fishermen ply their trade.

"When the men went out to tend their herring weirs, they'd stay overnight in small shacks sprinkled over the remote beaches and coves along the shores," Shirley begins. "They wanted to be there for the early morning tides because that's when the herring were running best and the nets would be full in no time."

It was in one of those small makeshift shacks on Chance Harbour that this story unfolds.

"As the story goes, one gentleman who used to live around here told of men who tried to spend the night at this particular camp. But no matter how many tried, they always left before the night was done. They always said it was haunted."

Now this particular gentleman, Shirley says, was a skeptic. He refused to believe the tales, which he described as nonsense.

"So this one night he decided to try it for himself. He got into bed and thought, *There's nothing wrong here. What's there to be afraid of?* A short while later, he awoke to the sounds of someone rowing and oars in the oarlocks. As a fisherman he knew the sounds very well. And it was a quiet night. There was no wind so there were few waves. He was sure he heard the sounds of someone rowing to the shore."

He assumed another fisherman was coming to stay for the night in order to be ready for the morning.

"Within minutes, the gentleman heard the distinct sounds of a small boat, maybe a dinghy, being pulled up on shore over the loose gravel to keep it from going adrift," Shirley continues. "Then he heard footsteps in the gravel as if someone was heading toward the cabin. Thinking he would see a fellow fisherman, this gentleman got up from bed, went to the door and opened it expecting to greet his visitor, but there was no one there."

Within minutes, according to Shirley's story, the gentleman packed up his belongings and left the shack, never to return. He was certain someone—or something—had walked up to the shack.

Did he hear the sounds of a phantom fisherman coming to shore that night? No one really knows for sure, but Shirley points out that after word of this incident spread throughout the village, no one would ever go back to that shack for more than a brief stop.

The Screeching Bridge

Parrsboro, Nova Scotia, is the largest town on the Minas Basin. It is favoured by rock hounds, who come to the area to search the beaches and cliffs for rocks such as agate and amethyst.

In 1985, the biggest fossil find in North America was unearthed on the north shore of the Minas Basin near Parrsboro. The discovery consisted of more than 100,000 pieces of 200-million-year-old fossils. The first such discovery made in North America, it was also the first collection unearthed in a series of dinosaur footprints, each the size of a penny (the smallest ever discovered).

The Minas Basin boasts some of the world's highest tides, and their dramatic effect on shipping can be seen from the Parrsboro wharf when fishing boats and other vessels are left stranded by the low tide. At high tide, water fills the harbour and reaches the small creek that runs under the town's main street.

The legend of Glooscap lives along this path of high tides, semi-precious stones and million-year-old fossils. Glooscap ruled the Mi'kmaq long before the white man arrived with his power to control the mighty tides of Fundy—or so the story goes. Legend says Glooscap created the Fundy tides and scattered the gems (his grandmother's jewellery) along the Minas Shore.

According to local folklore collector Conrad Byers, Parrsboro is also home to the famous Screeching Bridge.

"It is said that on the first snowfall of every winter season, you supposedly can hear screeching on the bridge if you dare to go across it at night," Conrad says. "According to the story, the bridge got its name because a woman committed suicide many, many years ago by throwing herself off the bridge. It just happened to be during the first snowfall of the season."

The story also says that the woman chose to end her life because she had a broken heart. "It seems the woman had fallen for a young local man and for whatever reason—no one really knows for sure—they couldn't be together. If she couldn't be with him, she didn't want to be with anyone."

Halifax's Haunted Hill

From its founding in 1749 until the end of the 19th century, Halifax was one of four principal overseas naval stations in the British Empire. To defend Halifax, British military authorities built a series of fortifications in and around the strategic port—a system now known as the Halifax Defence Complex.

By far the most impressive part of the system is the storied and protean Citadel. According to Parks Canada, the present Citadel, completed in 1856, is the fourth in a series of forts to occupy the hill overlooking the harbour. It is an excellent example of a 19th-century bastion fortification, complete with defensive ditch, ramparts, musketry gallery, powder magazine and signal masts. Although never attacked, the fort was garrisoned by the British Army until 1906 and by the Canadian Forces during the First and Second World Wars.

The fourth Citadel was established to guard against a land-based attack from the United States. The massive, star-shaped masonry fortification took 28 years to build. Constructed originally as a smooth-bore fortification, the

Citadel quickly became obsolete with the introduction of powerful rifles in the 1860s. In response to the rapidly changing times, the Citadel upgraded its armaments. Because the new artillery fired heavier shells a greater distance and with greater accuracy, the stronghold could defend the harbour and the mainland.

The major role for the Citadel in the early 1900s was to provide barrack accommodations and to act as a command centre for other harbour defences. When the Second World War broke out in 1939, the Citadel was used as temporary barracks for troops going overseas and as the centre for anti-aircraft operations in Halifax. The Citadel was the "last view of the country for so many thousands outward bound and the first landmark to those who returned."

Today, the Citadel is operated by Parks Canada and is recognized as one of the most important historic sites in Canada. The area has been restored with a living history program featuring the 78th Highland Regiment, the Royal Artillery, the soldiers' wives and civilian tradespeople. A visit to the Citadel is an educational and enjoyable heritage experience. Guided tours, an audiovisual presentation and modern exhibits reflect the Citadel's significance in Canadian history. If you're lucky, you just might encounter one of the many ghosts that are said to roam the hills, moats and ramparts.

Nova Scotia researcher George Munroe points out it is only natural that the Citadel, with its rich history, would be the location for a ghost story or two. "When you're dealing with a piece of land that has seen so much history and has been witness to the occasional tragedy, then I think it's natural

A historic site of national significance, Halifax's Citadel is also home to spirits that roam the ramparts and casemates of the fortification.

that some of those spirits would still wander the hills that protect the Citadel," he says.

Although George admits that he has never seen a ghost there, he tells of an incident in the mid-1960s when he was working as a summer interpreter and a fellow employee reported having a brush with the paranormal. "Of course we had heard all the stories of the soldiers and other ghosts haunting the Citadel, but unless you believe in that sort of thing, you're not likely to accept such stories," he continues, adding that he is a believer.

"It was said that in Halifax in 1855 there was a strong earthquake and part of the Citadel wall collapsed as the foundations were not deep enough. A roll call following the earthquake revealed one of the soldiers was missing. Despite an extensive search of the fortress and even the rubble from the fallen wall, the missing soldier was never found."

Several years later, the soldier was found in a well on the Citadel grounds. There are three very deep wells on the grounds. When the wells were still being used, soldiers had to clean them every five years. It was during one of those cleanings several years after the earthquake that the body of the missing soldier was found. He must have fallen in during the earthquake, never to be seen or heard from again. After his body was found, some people at the Citadel saw a ghostly image of a man walking the ramparts that surround the fortress. Those who reported seeing the man said he was dressed in a uniform from the 78th Regiment.

"One night, while I was working, I heard a commissioner making a commotion," George says. "The guy was a wreck and in a real panic. He told me that he had seen the ghost of a soldier dressed in a uniform. He said he knew it had been a ghost because the man was there one minute and gone the next. He said the image was kind of transparent as if he could look through him."

George asked the other fellow where he had seen the ghost and the man indicated over casemate 18, which was directly above the well where the soldier's body had been discovered.

"I'm not really sure what he saw that night," George says. "But it was clear he saw something. He was shaken up pretty badly."

Glenn Coolen of Halifax Ghost Walks says that while details of the Citadel ghosts vary from source to source, he too has heard the tales.

For example, he tells the story of a ghost "who walks the casemates of the recognizable landmark." The theory is that it is the ghost of a man who "stumbled into the moat one night and drowned following a night on the town."

Although many people have supposedly seen this ghost, Glenn says details are sparse at best.

Swinging in the Breeze

Records show that four locations in Halifax were used as gallows for public hangings—one by the willow tree at the corner of Robbie Street and Quinpool Road, one behind the old law courts (which is the last location where a public hanging took place in Nova Scotia) and one just above the stairs to the Grand Parade. The last remaining location was the site of the first gallows in the city's history and it is the spot of the original landing of Halifax. Today, that spot is the corner of Bedford Row and George Street, adjacent to an art gallery and facing the ferry terminal.

Glenn Coolen of Halifax Ghost Walks says, "That's where the waterline used to be hundreds of years ago when the first settlers arrived. When Edward Cornwallis and his band of fellow explorers stepped off their vessels in 1749, that was their landing point. The waterline has gone down about 500 metres, but Cornwallis and the others landed there because it was a very broad cove."

As the settlers made their way to shore and set up an encampment, they made note of an enormous hardwood tree on the shore. "They were impressed with the large oak tree on the water's edge and they appointed it as the first gallows in the new city."

In no time at all, they put it to use.

"It didn't take long for a young man by the name of Peter Cartell to put that tree to test," Glenn says. "If it was his intention to see how well the tree worked as gallows, he achieved his goal. It was in the year 1750 that Mr. Cartell went afoul of the floating provincial government of the day."

According to the story, the events occurred on the ship *Bowfort* as she was anchored in the harbour. "It seems Mr. Cartell stabbed three men, killing one of them. For his crimes, he was sentenced to and did in fact hang from that big old oak tree on the water's edge."

Today, local superstition states that on certain nights, at that spot right beside the doors of the art gallery, you can see a young man hanging by his neck and swinging in the breeze.

The Vanishing Ship

Unless people experience something for themselves, they tend to discredit phenomena that cannot easily be explained. Conrad Byers, a teacher and historian from Parrsboro, Nova Scotia, says that while he has always accepted that there are many mysteries in life that defy easy explanation, he personally has experienced some phenomena firsthand and even to this day wonders what exactly he saw.

He says it was in the early 1980s. He lived in Parrsboro but in a home closer to the harbour than where he lives today. It was late at night when it happened, not long after he had gone to bed.

"My girlfriend and I were asleep when I was woken by a ship's whistle, which was unusual to hear where I lived," Conrad says. "It was also odd because the whistle was from a larger vessel, which was unusual as there weren't too many freighters or large ships in this area."

Conrad has been around the sea for a great part of his life and he knows that five or more blasts of a ship's horn means there's trouble on board. In most cases, it means a fire or engine trouble. "Upon hearing the whistle, I immediately thought there was trouble. I could hear it, but I couldn't see it from my window. I said to my girlfriend, 'There's a ship out there in trouble.' We got dressed, got in the car and drove down to the harbour, which was about a mile from my house. There, we could get a clear view of the bay. It was dark, but we could see the lights."

At a glance, Conrad says, he could tell the ship appeared to be hung up around a place known to locals as Partridge Island. "I could see a freighter silhouetted against the dark skyline. It seemed to be right up on the island as if it had hit there and was grounded. There was a ship there. There's no question about that. Both my girlfriend and I saw it."

And it's a good thing, Conrad says, that he had a witness.

Just as anyone would do, Conrad reported the grounded ship to the authorities, who immediately launched a search for the troubled vessel. Despite an extensive search, nothing was ever found to indicate there had been a ship in distress that night. If Conrad hadn't had a witness with him that night—his girlfriend—the authorities most likely would have charged him with reporting a hoax.

Conrad says he is at a loss to explain the lights and the ship that they had seen, as well as the whistle that awakened him. After checking around his neighbourhood, he found that no one else had heard the whistle.

To this day, the incident remains a mystery.

4

Wandering Women

Black Betsy

The town of St. Andrews is in the southwest corner of New Brunswick on scenic Passamaquoddy Bay. Settled by Loyalists after the American Revolution, St. Andrews today continues to reflect the dominant themes of Loyalist social order—peace, order and stability. St. Andrews enjoys dynamic tourism and hospitality industries, as well as thriving eco-tourism, which includes sea kayaking and whale watching. It's also well known for its ghosts and other supernatural phenomena.

Elaine Bruff, operator of Heritage Discovery Tours of St. Andrews Ghost Walks, says the stories could be connected to the town's rich Loyalist heritage or simply to someone's overactive imagination. Either way, the town is full of ghost stories, including the story of Black Betsy.

Black Betsy wasn't a ghost, really, Elaine says. She was a witch, but she makes for a good tale nonetheless.

The legend goes that Black Betsy lived in St. Andrews in the mid-1800s. Back then, 18 wharves lined the town's waterfront, which plays a prominent role in the story of the mysterious woman.

It isn't clear if people gave Black Betsy her name because she was dark-skinned or because they thought she was a witch. But as Elaine tells the story, one day Black Betsy "was walking along the shores of St. Andrews where all the shipbuilding was taking place. As she was walking, she came upon a ship being built called the *Black Swan*." Near the wharves she began to pick up "small pieces of scrap wood, not really good enough for anything other than firewood, perhaps."

According to Elaine, the legend goes that as the diminutive woman began collecting the wood, the owner of the *Black Swan* started yelling at her and calling her horrible names. He chased the woman away, making her drop the wood as she ran.

As Black Betsy left, she said to the owner, "Sir, alls I'm doing is collecting little pieces of wood so that I can warm myself by the fire."

The ship's owner would hear none of this and continued to call the woman horrible names. As she turned to leave, she said to him, "Sir, for your rudeness, your ship will never go down the way."

He laughed as the woman left, thinking her claim was audacious and ridiculous.

The day came for the *Black Swan* to be launched. It was a glorious day in St. Andrews. The launching of a new ship was a significant event for the town in those days.

With the local residents and dignitaries gathered on the wharves and along the shores, the men released the scaffoldings, expecting the *Black Swan* to glide down the slip and into the bay like countless other vessels before her. But she wouldn't move.

The men pulled. They tugged. They tried everything, but nothing caused the ship to move. Eventually, several of the men who had been there the day Black Betsy had been sent away by the ship's owner said he had better call for the old woman.

The ship's owner, unaccustomed to believing in curses, said, "I don't believe. I will not send for her. Now get my ship down the way."

But after the shipyard workers could not get the ship to move, the owner finally relented and sent for Black Betsy.

She came to the wharf without hesitation. Looking at the wealthy owner, she asked, "Can I help you, sir? What is it you want from me today?"

He replied, "Can you let my ship go down the way?"

Black Betsy put her hand in the air and said, "If you cover my hand in gold, I will do that."

Still skeptical, but anxious to get his new ship in the water, the owner put a small bit of gold in her hand, but the ship did not budge. He then put another piece in the woman's hand, but the ship still did not move.

As the man continued to put gold in the woman's hand, the ship began to drift down the way until she finally splashed into the bay and Black Betsy left with her handful of gold.

Regardless of the story's veracity, Elaine says Black Betsy is well documented in the journals of the *Black Swan*. "There is no doubt that such a woman did exist. She was a local resident of St. Andrews. It is said she was a kind lady, if you were kind to her. But if you were unkind, then she was unkind to you. It's a safe bet that no one messed with Black Betsy after the *Black Swan* incident."

The Lady in Blue

Besides its iconic lighthouse, Peggy's Cove, Nova Scotia, is known for rugged granite headlands where the Atlantic Ocean crashes onto shore. This granite is estimated to be more than 415 million years old. The last retreating glaciers picked up and randomly deposited huge boulders in the area 10,000 years ago. Peggy's Cove has also been the site of many tragedies, the most recent being Swissair Flight 111, which plunged into the icy cold waters on the night of September 2, 1998, killing all 229 people on board.

As with other Maritime communities, Peggy's Cove is also known for its ghost stories. One of the most notable concerns the Lady in Blue. The story was told to me by resident artist Donna Maquire, who operates a studio, Rogue Gallery, not far from the famous lighthouse. With its psychic undertones, Donna says, the story of the Lady in Blue is more about a vision than a ghost.

Many people have reported seeing the Lady in Blue on the granite rocks at Indian Harbour, a small outport less than a mile from Peggy's Cove. Donna explains: "The story goes that she was actually a Scottish lady who met and married a man from Indian Harbour during the First World War. Returning to Nova Scotia, the couple settled down and had nine children, but apparently the woman was never happy. It was believed that she suffered from what we would call post-partum depression. Finally, after years of struggling to find happiness at Peggy's Cove, the distraught woman gave up and headed back to Scotland on a steamliner out of Halifax. She left her children behind with their father."

Sadly, the woman never made it back to her homeland. The ship reportedly sank off the coast of Scotland and

A ghost known as the Lady in Blue haunts Indian Harbour near Peggy's Cove, Nova Scotia.

many of the passengers, including the woman, drowned. Shortly thereafter, local residents reported seeing the vision of a woman in a blue dress walking the rocks of Indian Harbour. According to Donna, some people actually heard her speaking as she glided across the granite.

"I'm sorry," the woman reportedly says. "I'm sorry for leaving you."

The locals concluded that this was the Lady in Blue expressing remorse for abandoning her children. She had returned to look for them.

There is another version of the story in which the woman left her children behind in Nova Scotia after her husband drowned while fishing and she couldn't look after them on her own. In this version, the couple have four children. Donna says she is more inclined to believe this story than the first one.

"I got to know one of the older residents of the community quite well. She's dead now, but she told me the story of how her mother had come to Indian Harbour as a war bride during the First World War. She didn't fit in with the locals and they didn't like her. Apparently, after her husband drowned while fishing, she just wasted away by herself in this small village where she was like an outcast. Locals said they often saw the tall, thin, brown-haired woman walking up and down the rocks at Indian Harbour. Oh, and yes, she did wear a blue dress very often."

In this version, the woman's family in Scotland managed to scrape up enough money to bring her home. She left her children with her late husband's family who raised them. The woman never saw her children again.

Donna says the details in the two stories are very similar, but following an experience with a psychic friend who visited her a few years ago from Toronto, she became convinced the second version is more true.

"One day, my friend from Toronto who has psychic abilities went for a walk on the rocks at Indian Harbour. She was gone for a while but when she came back she looked strange and quickly asked me if someone had died here. I said, of course. It's a fishing village. A lot of people have died around here. No, my friend said. Did a woman die here?"

Donna says she immediately recalled the story that the elderly woman had told her and quickly relayed the details to her friend, who then insisted that she meet the older woman. During the course of their conversation, Donna says she was astounded as her friend from Toronto described, in detail, the elderly woman's mother, right down to a ring on her finger.

Had her psychic friend seen the ghost of the older woman's dead mother on the rocks that day? Donna admits that she can't say for sure, but she is certain that her friend had made some kind of connection to the spirit world.

The Headless Nun

The mighty Miramichi River in northern New Brunswick is world renowned for its salmon. The city of Miramichi was formed through the amalgamation of five municipal units and several rural areas in 1995. Its population is estimated at almost 19,500, making it the fourth largest city in the province. English is the dominant language of the local residents, while about 19 percent indicate knowledge of both English and French.

Its French connection gives Miramichi one of the Maritimes' most intriguing ghost stories.

According to Jeff Clark, a summer student at French Fort Cove, the story dates back to the late 1750s when a nun was supposedly killed.

The story goes that Sister Marie Inconnus was killed one evening while she was returning to the Acadian settlement at French Fort Cove after helping a Mi'kmaq woman through a difficult childbirth. It is said that as she passed the bridge that crossed over the Ruisseau a Corneille (now known as Cow Brook), two madmen who had escaped from a nearby leprosy colony attacked her.

The two deranged men were in search of a treasure that was believed to be buried somewhere in the cove, and only Sister Marie knew of its location. The booty was said to be jewellery and bits of gold brought to the wild frontier by the early settlers. The men hoped to buy passage back to their native country. Although severely beaten, the nun refused to divulge the whereabouts of the treasure. In a fit of rage, one of the men is said to have severed Sister Marie's head with his sword. Her head was thrown into the waters of the cove while her body was left on the bridge.

The French troops who found the nun's body the next day ensured that it was returned to her homeland to be buried in the family crypt. Her head was never recovered.

The story of Sister Marie's tragic death became folklore, handed down from one generation to the next. It is said that without her head, the nun is unable to rest in peace. Many believe she still haunts the cove, terrifying all those who hear her plea, "Please find my head and return it to my body and set my soul free." It is also reputed that Sister Marie's headless form offers to pay a handsome reward to those who help her.

As for the treasure of French Fort Cove, it remains a mystery. Anyone who goes looking for it is said to be greeted by its guardian—the Headless Nun.

Surprisingly, Jeff says, many people believe her story.

"People around here have said they've seen the ghost," he says. "We've heard people tell stories of seeing the nun walking around without her head and crying out for someone to help her find it. One guy who was riding on horseback was supposedly thrown when his horse refused to cross the bridge. It's said the nun followed another guy all the way home from the bridge and stood beside his bed asking him to help find her head."

According to Jeff, the story stipulates that if someone helps Sister Marie find her head, she will guide them to the treasure.

But be warned.

The Mysterious Cassie Smith

Shelburne County, on Nova Scotia's picturesque South Shore, is noted for its strange tales of haunts and witchcraft. Many of the early settlers were French and brought their beliefs about the paranormal with them from their homeland.

The people in this seafaring community are kind, honest and hard-working. They tell their tales of peculiar events with great sincerity, and are prepared to back up the statements of their friends and neighbours as that of the gospel truth.

Marilyn Atwood, who grew up in Shelburne County, says that when she was a youngster, she had heard of mysterious things at the Smith place at Port Saxon, just a few miles from the friendly town of Shelburne. In search of ghost stories (to share with me), Marilyn recently went looking for and found Mrs. Jennie Harris, whom she describes as an intelligent, God-fearing elder of the community. Jennie advised Marilyn to seek out Richard Webber, who could clarify the story since his brother, Irvin, had lived in the haunted house after the Smith family moved out.

However, Marilyn says, before leaving to find Richard Webber, she had a nice long chat with the members of Jennie's family regarding the strange happenings at Port Saxon. Neil Webber, nephew of Richard, had been at the Smith home spending his summer vacation with his wife and family from the United States. He told of seeing strange lights crossing the sky when he was a youngster. This was clarified by Ephrian Harris, son of Jennie, who told of tying lights on long sticks and waving them back and forth in the air to frighten the residents when he was a boy.

When asked if he believed in ghosts, Ephrian replied, "No, not exactly…But I would like to know what I met on the bridge coming home from Port Saxon one night when I was a kid."

Ephrian explained that he had been returning home in a wagon with Raymond Stoddart one night in 1919. The horse was speedy and Stoddart was getting the most from it by flicking it on the rump with the whip. Suddenly, just as they reached the wooden bridge coming from town, the horse slowed down and seemed reluctant to proceed further onto the bridge. Just then, the young men heard the galloping hooves and the unmistakable clatter of another horse and wagon entering the bridge from the other end. Raymond coaxed his own horse to the side of the bridge and shouted to his companion, "My God, he's going to run us down."

As the two men waited for the second horse and wagon to come into view, the sound drew closer. Then, when the inevitable crash was about to take place in the darkness, the sounds of the horse and wagon ceased completely, leaving the two very frightened men cowering in their wagon on the bridge with a horse almost too nervous to move. Ephrian's father laughed at the boys—that is, until the phantom horse and wagon almost scared him out of his wits on the same bridge one night.

Reverend Chase of Port Saxon also received a jolt one night on the bridge. He saw the form of a young woman with no head who threw herself over the rail of the structure and plunged into the water below right before the eyes of the startled minister.

There was also the lady dressed completely in white who would be seen leading a flock of pure white geese across the highway at night, only to disappear without a trace of herself or her flock.

Marilyn did talk to Richard Webber and found him to be a friendly person who lost no time relating the mysterious story of Cassie Smith's ghost.

Joseph and Cassie Smith had seven children, one of whom was named Sarah. She moved to the United States in 1916 and was found shortly after hanging by the neck, the victim of an apparent suicide. It was generally believed that Sarah took her own life because of an impending shame—the birth of her illegitimate child. Her father, Joseph, was very saddened by the death of his daughter and angry because he believed his wife had known of the pregnancy and kept the information from him.

Time aggravated his anger and the ferocity of his fits of bad temper. Cassie could no longer bear the bad treatment that was heaped upon her by her irate husband. One morning she disappeared and was later found by her angry husband down by the calm river not far from the farm. Joseph marched Cassie home and, after much scolding, left her in her misery in the farmhouse while he went about his chores. That same morning, Cassie Smith ended her miserable existence by hanging herself over the threshing floor of the barn.

After that, strange things began to occur around the farm. Among other things, a horseless wagon was seen racing across the field near the barn. The reports continued until the Smiths moved away and Irvin Webber moved in. He immediately reported that strange things began happening.

One day, according to Irvin, while he was in the hayloft he heard a noise below on the threshing floor, as if someone was being strangled. He crawled over to the edge and looked down, but there was nothing there. Then he heard the strangling noise again, only from a different corner of the barn. Irvin thought it must have been the sound of the old lady hanging herself.

Richard Webber said he actually saw Cassie Smith after that. It was one foggy morning when his mother looked out of the window toward the Smith farm, then owned by Irvin.

"Come here," she called to Richard and the other children. "There's Cassie Smith if I ever saw her."

The children looked out and sure enough, there stood the old lady in the morning fog and mist with a black shawl over her shoulders and head. She soon disappeared as mysteriously as she had come.

"Another time," Richard said, "I was at Irvin's house with the girl who was later to become my wife. We were sitting in the kitchen and there was a bedroom off the kitchen. I swear the door kept opening. We would get up and close it, but each time the door would open again. No matter how many times we closed it, it would open. I also remember there was a lamp on the table with a big glass shade on it. All of a sudden, that lamp tipped up and up until it went crashing to the floor, but the table never moved a bit."

Another time, Richard says, "Irvin and I were down in the cellar making apple cider with a small cider mill when we heard footsteps upstairs, just like a man walking around. We knew there was nobody up there, but Irvin wasn't afraid of anything. He lifted the trapdoor leading from the cellar to the kitchen and hollered, 'I own this place now. Get the hell out of here and stay out.' We never heard the footsteps again that day."

Late one night, Richard Webber remembers returning home from an apple-peeling party (where apples are peeled, then strung out to dry for baking) when he saw the Smith house lit up from top to bottom. This was in the days of kerosene lamps. Richard knew the house was empty, since its occupants were still at the apple-peeling party. But, Richard says, just as suddenly as the lights had come on, they went out, leaving the house in complete darkness.

After Irvin Smith and his family moved out of the house, it sat vacant for several years until it burned down to the ground. It is believed the spirit of Cassie Smith finally found some peace after her place of torment was destroyed. Her ghost has never again haunted the community of Port Saxon.

The Haunted Pool

Many years ago, it is said, a farmer objected strongly to his youngest daughter moving away from home to become a labourer in the big city. In his opinion, young girls alone in a city are exposed to many temptations and are apt to "go wrong." A year later, the farmer's gloomy predictions were confirmed. The girl returned to the farm, an unwed mother with an infant in her arms.

It was a wild, stormy night, but the father, beside himself with grief and rage, turned the unfortunate girl away and told her never to darken his doorstep again.

As the destitute creature wandered through the storm, she failed to realize how close she had come to the edge of a deep marshy pool that lay between the village road and her father's farm. The bank crumbled beneath her feet. Before she could stop herself, she had plunged into the deep water, which closed over the heads of both mother and child.

A few people later hinted that the young mother's plunge might have been intentional, but no one knew for sure. All that was for certain was that the two pathetic bodies were found and removed from the pool a few days later. The mother and baby were buried, as was the custom in those days, outside the inner sanctum of the village cemetery, but they were not forgotten. Word soon spread that their spirits walked among the living.

The unforgiving father was the first to see them. Returning home one night in the dark, he was horrified to see the ghost of his daughter, dressed as he had last seen her and with her baby in her arms, coming from the direction of the pool where she had drowned. She crossed silently in front of his horse in the lantern light and disappeared again into the blackness.

After that, the father began taking the long way around or using a different route to avoid passing near the haunted pool. But soon the phantom began to stand in his front yard and look at him with sad, reproaching eyes. Then, clutching her baby in her arms, she would turn and walk away into the darkness, just as she had done that fateful night when her father had sent her away.

Others beside the father soon began to see the ghosts. In time a legend grew and the pool was pointed out to strangers visiting the rural village. Long before the legend took hold, however, the father of the drowned girl, who had become a withdrawn recluse, took his own life.

The Ghost of Keenan Bridge

The story of the Keenan Bridge ghost in New Brunswick has been told throughout Carleton and Victoria Counties for many years. One of the area's residents, Ann Brennan (who is also a local historian), knows the stories that surround the famous covered bridge. Along with her daughter Rayanne Brennan and family friend Frances Cullen, she works to preserve the community's rich history, but also to protect and record the story of the Keenan Bridge ghost.

Of the ghost Ann says, "We see it as a positive thing for Johnville. We are always overwhelmed with the response we receive from people when we share this particular phenomenon."

To understand the story of Keenan Bridge, Ann insists you must first know the history of the bridge and the community as a whole. "This entire community was settled by the Irish and with them came the collective ideology of ghosts and other old country traditions," she writes in a brief history of the bridge.

Ann first came to the Johnville area some 40 years ago, and she recalls that right from the very beginning, she felt there was something special about Keenan Bridge and the area around it. "I felt the area was such a sad place and the local people insisted it was haunted. They would tell us not to go there at night because there were ghosts there. In the daytime, however, it was a peaceful and wonderful place where everyone gathered and the kids would swim. People would party there, so it became a community gathering place even though everyone knew it was haunted. It was still a place that everybody wanted to go to."

In the centre of this photograph, an image of a woman's face is said to hover over the smouldering remains of Keenan Bridge.

As rural people, Ann says, the residents of the farming communities were drawn to the area by the arability of the land. Even before Keenan Bridge was built, the people celebrated the richness of the surroundings. "It was a gathering place that held a certain mystery. It has to do with the energy coming from the river. The river makes nice sounds and there's lots of interesting things happening there with the wind and so on. The Irish would call it a sacred site because of the energy there and the collective weird things that happen there."

The wooden bridge that spanned Monquart Stream was built in 1927 to join the settlements of Killoween and Johnville. It was named after the first Keenan family, who were among the earliest settlers to arrive in Johnville from

Peterborough, Ontario, in the late 1860s. The Keenans—
along with the Cummings, Boyds and Hurleys—came in
response to Bishop Sweeney's solicitations for settlers to
take up early land grants. During the years that followed,
the bridge and the area became steeped in stories of the
supernatural, which Ann says included ghosts and stories of
mysterious occurrences, one of the most famous being the
ghost of Keenan Bridge.

At the turn of the last century, before the bridge was
built, a well-known and highly respected older lady disappeared from the community. It is said she was travelling
from her family home on one side of the river to the other
side when she disappeared. Despite a massive search of the
area, no clues were ever found as to the woman's whereabouts. Exactly what happened to the missing grandmother
remains a mystery.

As with any mysterious disappearance, there were many
theories about the woman's fate. But, Ann says, "her body or
any trace of her were never found. There's all kinds of local
whispers but we're not even sure if she is tied to the bridge.
When it was under construction, a skull was found where
they were trying to put in abutments. There was nothing
else—no body. It is said that the road construction super-
visor suggested to the workers that they should bury it. His
words were 'Bury it and bury it deep and don't ever
mention it again.'"

But, Ann quickly adds, the workers had to tell. It was a
good story.

It was shortly after Keenan Bridge was built that things
started happening. Some were mysterious while others were
orchestrated by young local men. "It was hard to separate
the ghosts from the realities but, make no mistake, there

were strange things happening there. As people went through the bridge, they sensed someone's presence. It was as if they were being accompanied by someone. This was particularly true if you were travelling alone."

In a written account of one well-known incident, Ann recounts the story. "One of the most often recited stories concerns John Hurley, who passed through the bridge on his way to his sister's home on Christmas Eve. Suddenly John realized he had been joined in the sleigh by the form of a woman covered in a black shawl. The horses reared up in fear and went flying out of control down the road. When John reached his sister's home, he fell into the kitchen in a dead faint on the floor. It was some time before he was able to describe what had happened to him. He continued to maintain the truth of the story for the rest of his life."

According to local historians, the tale changes somewhat from one telling to the next, but the central elements are consistent. Ann says the story has become part of the community's traditions and legends. "The remarkable thing about this fellow was that even though he was in a state of shock, he described the ghostly woman very well. She was a lady dressed in period costume and it was black. She merely accompanied him across the bridge."

Some years later, the story of the mysterious woman who appeared on Keenan Bridge took on new meaning when some locals started telling tales of a headless ghost. But Ann says many historians attribute the stories to exaggeration stemming from the legend of the skull that had been discovered during the bridge's construction. "I'm not a hundred percent sure that anyone actually saw a headless ghost on the bridge. We have many stories of a ghostly woman accompanying people across the bridge, but so far as I know she had a head. And truth is, we're not even sure that the older woman who disappeared some 20 or 25 years before the bridge was built is even the ghost. We just don't know."

Over the years, and in more recent times, Keenan Bridge achieved a certain level of fame throughout the area because of the ghost stories. According to Ann, a group of local musicians named themselves Keenan Bridge and used a tune by the same title as their theme song. Their music brought recognition to the area and the bridge became a symbol of pride for the local inhabitants. The bridge is also the subject of many stories and poems. Unfortunately, the structure itself no longer stands. The community of Johnville suffered a great historic loss when the covered bridge burned down in the early hours of May 3, 2001. Many locals believe the destructive fire was the work of vandals, as several other fires were also discovered that night, but nothing has ever been proven.

This is where the story takes on a new and even more bizarre twist.

During the summer of 2001, area residents organized a celebration to commemorate the historic structure and to launch a fundraising campaign in support of any future efforts to rebuild the covered bridge. At a community picnic held that August, one of the local men who had responded to the early morning fire revealed some unusual photos he had taken immediately following the blaze. The man didn't develop the film for several months, but when he eventually saw the photos he was shocked to notice that several pictures of the bridge on fire contained the image of a woman's head and face in the middle of the smouldering ruins. There is no body. Just the head.

Naturally, Ann says, people's imaginations ran wild as stories of the image spread. "You have to judge the image for yourself, but there is no question that it looks like a woman's face in the photo."

Is it the image of the ghost who was said to haunt Keenan Bridge? Or is it that of the elderly woman who disappeared some one hundred years earlier while trying to cross the river, never to be seen again?

No one can say for sure, but Ann Brennan says with some conviction, "I still believe that whatever was there is still there and is still connected to our community."

Today, a new single strand bridge, completed in July 2001, crosses the river. Although Keenan Bridge is gone, many locals believe the ghost is still with them.

5
Local
Legends

The Curse of the Wedding Dress

On the corner of Hollis and Sackville Streets in Halifax stands a building that was erected in the 1850s by a woman entrepreneur. Her business was well-known for its dry goods, most notably clothing. The woman specialized in ladies' clothing, particularly gowns. The store's reputation spread far and wide. Everyone who was anyone shopped there, especially young women seeking the perfect gown for their wedding days.

Glenn Coolen of Halifax Ghost Walks says around the same time there was a pretty young woman down West Dublin way. West Dublin was a small fishing village on the province's South Shore. It would take a three-day voyage on a sleek schooner to get from there to Halifax and back again. The girl, Angela Publicover, was engaged to be married to a young sailor from the community. Everyone said it was a perfect match and they would live happily ever after.

The year was 1858 and Angela had been to Halifax before to attend a wedding. On that occasion, she had been awestruck by the beauty and grace of the elaborate wedding gowns worn by the young city brides. If she was to be married, then she must be married in a gown such as theirs. Angela decided she would be the first girl from West Dublin to wear such a gown. She would sail back to Halifax, go to the dress store where the city brides purchased their gowns and then return to her community to be married in grand style. It would be a beautiful wedding and the gown would be the icing on the cake.

The store turned out to be the building on the corner of Sackville and Hollis. The building sits empty today, but in its time it was said to have been a grand place. As Glenn tells the story, "It was October or November when Angela set out on her journey. Her fiancé, her friends and her family had all tried to convince Angela not to go until the spring because the ocean could be mean at that time of year. But Angela wouldn't listen to them. She wanted a nice gown like a city bride and she intended to have one. She hopped on board a tiny schooner called the *Industry* and set sail for Halifax."

In good weather, the journey would normally take three days, round trip. It took Angela six months.

"You see, the *Industry* wound up in the middle of a storm at the mouth of the harbour. Since it was a rocky coastline, the captain decided to take his chances further out on the sea to escape the rocks. It was a fateful miscalculation as the ship sailed directly into the fierce storm. The ship's riggings were destroyed. The sails were badly torn. The ship was damaged beyond repair, becoming unnavigable. The crew of the *Industry* and Angela Publicover found themselves floating in the middle of the Atlantic Ocean without command of the ship or the ability to communicate with anyone else."

The situation looked grim and hopeless. There was a limited supply of food, fresh water and other stores on board, so they were in dire straits.

"Several weeks later, when everyone was at the point of starvation, Angela and the crew of the *Industry* were picked up by a steamer which was heading from Boston to London, England. Angela and the others were rescued, but the captain of the steamer was on business and didn't want to return to Halifax, so he took his rescued passengers with him all the way to England. Angela was now way off course and off schedule. She had planned to be gone only a few days and she had already been gone for months."

Undaunted, Angela sought out another ship that could provide her passage home.

"She found another steamer heading back to Nova Scotia, so she hopped on board and made her return to Halifax. Once she got to Halifax, she went to the dress shop, purchased the gown and caught another schooner back to West Dublin six months after she left home."

Of course, the entire village was happy to see Angela Publicover. They had long ago given her and all the others on board the *Industry* up for dead. They rejoiced in Angela's return and she, in turn, celebrated her good fortune. But the celebrations would not last long.

"Upon her return, Angela discovered the tragic news that her fiancé had been killed in the very same storm that had taken her so far from home. In such superstitious times, the people of West Dublin sought a scapegoat and realized that the one thing that stood out about the story was the wedding dress. The people in the small village were convinced that a curse had been placed on the wedding dress."

Although they insisted that the dress must be destroyed, Angela refused, vowing to keep it as a memorial to her lost love. With that, then, the villagers forbade any young woman from West Dublin ever to wear the accursed dress.

"Angela's wedding dress would have remained a local superstition unless another young woman, also engaged to a young sailor, hadn't come along several years later. She had heard the story of Angela Publicover's cursed gown, but she didn't believe it. She was determined to wear the dress. Her fiancé and her family and friends tried unsuccessfully to convince her not to wear the dress because of the curse. Nevertheless, the young lady was convinced she should. She tried it on; it fit perfectly. She decided then and there that she would wear the gown despite all the warnings."

Within days, the villagers faced yet another tragedy.

"A few days after taking the dress home, this young woman's husband-to-be was killed in a terrible storm out on the Atlantic. She was devastated and withdrew from the other villagers. In a desperate act of grief, the young woman put on the dress and refused to take it off. She would not wear anything but the dress. And in the days following her fiancé's death, the young woman never again spoke to a single living soul in West Dublin."

Tragic as it is, the story doesn't end there.

"One day, some time following the tragedy, the young woman in the wedding gown wandered out of West Dublin, never again to be seen by anyone from the village. Days passed and there was no word of her whereabouts until a foreign fishing vessel came into port and moored alongside the landing at West Dublin. The captain and crew reported what they had just seen in the middle of the harbour. As they were sailing in, they had seen a figure in a white dress floating just a few feet below the surface. When they went over to see what it was, the figure in white dipped down in the water beyond their view."

Although they admitted they had not clearly seen the figure, all on board insisted that the figure was wearing a white wedding dress.

"The residents of West Dublin believed the story and they were relieved to learn that the cursed wedding dress was at the bottom of the Atlantic Ocean, where it belonged. It could no longer steal away any of their young people."

The Ghost of New River Beach

New River Beach, in the southernmost reaches of New Brunswick, has some of the most intriguing and picturesque beaches in the country, highlighted by the Bay of Fundy, one of the marine wonders of the world.

Visitors to this natural wonderland discover a panorama of small islands, fishing boats and wildlife. Gulls, elder ducks and cormorants nest offshore and along the many trails. There are large tidal pools for crab, periwinkles, welks and starfish. In addition to all this natural beauty, ghosts are said to haunt the beach and a few of the neighbouring homes.

From his home in Saint John, storyteller David Goss collects and shares eerie tales. He has gathered many accounts about the ghost of New River. Although the details are sketchy at best, he has written a newspaper article about the eerie events.

David says the story goes back more than a century to when the Saxby Gale helped to sink the barque *Genii* on October 6, 1869, with the loss of 11 lives. The bodies of the sailors were taken up to a cottage overlooking the beach. There, the sailors were laid out in the living room until the buckboards could come up from Mascarene, below St. George, to retrieve them for burial. Apparently, some of the sailors still return to the house and wander about. Noises will be heard late at night and sometimes a half body, legs only, will be seen ascending the stairs.

Some have said they have been warned not to disturb the ghosts in the valley behind the house, where the outfall of the New River dashes over the smooth ledges and into the Bay of Fundy. Some people believe that on moonlit nights in Deadman's Cove on the Barnaby Trail, just east of the beach, a ghost appears. Local storytellers insist that it was the *Genii* tragedy that gave Deadman's Cove its name, but few people have gone there on a moonlit night to find out if it's haunted.

There are more stories connected to the beach. One tells of a slave woman chained with her child in the basement of a house that burned to the ground on St. John Road near where a school stands today. Some claim the ghostly woman's screams and clanking chains are still heard by those who walk along the road at night.

Lloyd Mealey of Pocologan, now deceased, shared the following story with David.

"My grandfather used to live on Davis' Point. At that time it was called Mealey's Point. He liked to shoot ducks, so one day he rowed out to New River Island, quite close to the shore, where he stood up in his small dinghy to load his gun. In those days, they loaded them with powder.

"His relatives were on the point watching him when he fell overboard. They said, 'Don't worry about him, he's a good swimmer,' but he never came up. A week or two later, they caught a shark in the Patch Weir at McCarthy's Point. They took it ashore, opened it up and found human hair in its gullet the same colour as my grandfather's, so they were sure the shark must have come up under the boat, knocked him overboard and probably eaten him."

Lloyd had another interesting story to relate to David. "Arthur Farquharson and his companion saw a ghost on New River Beach. They were driving down Carrying Cove when they both looked over to where our sardine weir was. They saw a woman wading along the water's edge. It was nearly low tide. She had a long white housecoat on and looked like she was wading in about six to eight inches of water. Arthur said to his companion, 'Did you see what I saw?' and he said, 'Yes.'"

The two men decided to drive over to see who the woman was. When they got there, she was gone.

In the days that followed, according to what Lloyd told David, several other local men reported seeing the woman in the white housecoat. Since no one was ever able to find her when they went to investigate, they assumed she was a ghost.

Strange Happenings at Vengeance House

The following excerpt by Beatrice M. Haw Shaw, first published by the *Yarmouth Times* in 1903, was reprinted in the *Sunday Leader* in 1921.

"I have fond memories of Yarmouth, having been stationed there for quite some time during the Second World War, where I served as an infantry instructor and I was delighted to find these excellent accounts of the incident which occurred in the town in a house at the head of Marshall Lane."

The story takes place in the early 19th century in an inn called Vengeance House, originally built by a Captain Rechman. He was a seafaring man and had served as midshipman on the battleship *Vengeance*. The captain was a man of "parts" (i.e., well travelled) and he was quite versatile with the brush, for the sign which he had painted and hung over the inn was considered noteworthy by art critics. As an ex-naval man, it followed that his inn should be the meeting place for seamen and military men who visited or lived in the town.

Captain Rechman had one son and a daughter named Lydia, whose closest friend was a 15-year-old girl named Maria. She lived with her family near Vengeance House, and the two girls spent much time together.

An elderly religious man, Captain Neale of Salem, Massachusetts, also lived at the inn. Neale had seen a great deal of the world and was a man of intelligence and sound judgment. He was not one to accept things without a thorough investigation.

One night, Maria slept over at the inn. The next morning, just after the girls had awakened, they heard a gentle tapping at the head of the bed. The two listened intently. Again they heard it. Tap, tap it went. They decided it was someone in the inn tapping, so they paid little attention. From that moment, the tapping never left them. It was always with them whenever Maria was present.

Eventually the girls became concerned about the strange tapping sounds following them, and they spoke to the others at Vengeance House. The guests attributed the sounds to rats and paid little heed. Captain Neale swore that it was some devilment that the girls had cooked up and that he would discover the source.

On a Sunday two weeks later, Captain Rechman was in bed and Mrs. Rechman, her son, her daughter and Maria were up and about the house. The girls were making a great deal of noise. Mrs. Rechman objected to the their laughter on the Sabbath and spoke to them quite sharply.

The two girls took a candle and went up to the bedroom directly over the kitchen. They put out the light after getting into bed. The tapping began immediately. It was loud and rapid, and seemed to be coming from the floor, ceiling and mantle. The girls became alarmed and called to Mrs. Rechman to bring a light. The woman thought that they were acting up again and warned them to be quiet or suffer the consequences.

The girls' fright, however, was genuine, and they kept screaming for Mrs. Rechman to come to their aid with the candle. She finally did and noticed that the girls were frightened to the point of hysteria. Mrs. Rechman called her husband to the scene. After listening for some time, he began to tear the ceiling off in search of the rats that he believed were making the noise.

When the ceiling came off, it made no difference—the tapping continued coming from everywhere.

In time, the tapping ceased except in Lydia's room, but poor little Maria was haunted wherever she went. Soon she was terrified to be alone. The story travelled far and wide, and the inn was beset with visitors who wished to hear the "ghosts." But Captain Neale refused to believe the story and offered $500 of his own money to anyone who could explain how the trick was done.

Every means was tried to discover the trickery of the girls. They were even isolated on a wooden bench off the floor, but still the knocking continued—so loudly and fiercely, in fact, that it seemed the floor and ceiling would surely break. Next the girls were placed on a pile of feather beds. Still the knocking persisted.

Then a code was devised and questions were put to the "ghost" using the code. Sensible questions were answered by a series of knocks. Foolish ones were answered by scratching sounds, showing that the "thing" responsible was of some intelligence. Doctors, ministers and lawyers were called in to ask questions in code that an average person would not be able to answer. The correct answers were given.

Once, a well-known captain was at port waiting for favourable weather for sailing. He appealed to the "thing" for information.

"When can I leave?" he asked.

There was no answer.

"Am I going to die?" the captain asked.

Still there was no answer.

But the captain persisted and asked the following questions: "How many years will I live? How many months? How many weeks?"

There was no answer to any of them.

When the captain said, "How many days?" there were three distinct knocks, which caused the man to chuckle. Three days later, while still waiting to sail, he dropped dead in the street.

Some suggested that the voice might wish to communicate with Maria; the answer was "yes."

For some time, Maria's brother had been missing at sea and was thought to have been murdered by pirates. When she asked if this was true, the answer came, "yes," but she would not remain alone to learn the identity of the guilty party. When the "thing" was asked if the information would come to both Lydia and Maria in human voice, six knocks answered, but the girls refused to follow up on the portent.

The strain began to show on Maria and she became weak and sick. She began to lose weight from not eating, and her relatives, fearing the girl would become seriously ill, refused her permission to return to Vengeance House again. From that time on, the knocking ceased to annoy her and she began to recover. With the fear gone, she acted like her old self once again.

Six months later, Maria was at the home of a Yarmouth family by the name of Marshall. She was sitting in an easy chair talking to family members. Suddenly she screamed that a snake was twisting up her leg; she went limp with fright. The snake quickly uncoiled from her left leg and went "rap, rap, rap" when it disappeared under an old desk across the room. The startled members of the household frantically searched for the reptile, moving furniture in the room and scouring every nook and cranny, but the snake was never found. From that day forth, Maria was never bothered again by the tapping.

Although Maria's experiences were big news in the small Nova Scotia town, most people were incapable of explaining them. The events are equally inexplicable today.

The Ghost Road

The town of St. Andrews, in the southwest corner of New Brunswick, is connected to the province's largest city, Saint John, by Route 127. Off Route 127, another road connects St. Andrews to another town, St. Stephen. Local residents call it the Ghost Road.

Elaine Bruff, who runs Heritage Discovery Tours of St. Andrews Ghost Walks, explains. "Coming into St. Andrews from Saint John, the road makes a wild curve just before it gets to the town. That's where you get on the road to St. Stephen. It's called the Ghost Road because the people of the area believe it to be haunted."

Elaine says there are a couple of ghost stories connected to the road.

"That happens in a small community. Someone hears something and passes it along. By the time the story makes its rounds, it's nothing like the original. One of the most famous stories connected with the Ghost Road is about a hitchhiker who disappears when he's offered a ride. The story goes back to the early 1800s when the road was being laid."

Two men were making their way to St. Andrews. They stopped just outside of town to work on the road because construction jobs paid good money for the times. They befriended the locals and it wasn't long before they met a pretty young girl and both fell in love with her. Both young men courted the local girl until she was forced to choose one over the other. The one who wasn't chosen was very angry. One night, while the two lovers were sitting on a rock near the road, the relationship ended with bloodshed. The spurned man came upon his friend and the young girl. He lost his temper and in a fit of jealous anger he murdered his friend.

Today, it is said that if you are going along the road at night you might see a man hitchhiking toward St. Andrews. If you stop to pick him up, he disappears. Locals believe the mysterious hitchhiker is the ghost of the murdered friend trying to complete his journey to St. Andrews.

"I know this one girl," Elaine says, "who grew up near the road. She believes very strongly that the road is haunted. When she was a young girl, she had a friend who lived farther up the road and she'd visit her quite often. Whenever she was walking home, she always felt a presence, like someone was watching her. One day while she was walking home, she was startled to encounter a man dressed in older clothing standing beside the road and waving at her, as if beckoning her to join him. The girl became alarmed as she knew this man was not from the community. Picking up speed, she quickly headed for home but then, in an instant, the man was gone."

When the girl's neighbours heard the story, they insisted she had seen the ghost of the man who had been murdered there many decades earlier.

Another theory about the spirit that haunts the Ghost Road is that it is the ghost of an Indian maiden who was hit by a carriage as she was walking. While reports of her ghost are not as numerous as those of the mysterious traveller, many local residents insist the Indian maiden haunts the road. They say that when you walk the road alone at night, you can hear her crying off in the woods as if she might be injured.

What really haunts the road between St. Andrews and St. Stephen? No one really knows for sure, but the locals—who still believe the stories are true—call it the Ghost Road to this day.

The Ghost of Dunbar Hill

Off the coast of St. Andrews, New Brunswick, is Campobello Island. Perhaps best known as the getaway retreat for American President Franklin D. Roosevelt, the island is also said to have a ghost.

Like the previous story, this one is told by Elaine Bruff, operator of Heritage Discovery Tours of St. Andrews Ghost Walks. The story hearkens back to the days of the town's early Loyalist settlers, a time when thieves and lawbreakers were handled with harsh laws and stiff penalties, often ending with hanging. It was common in those times for most towns to have their own gallows, and St. Andrews was no different. Commissioned by the British government, a Mr. Dunbar from nearby Campobello Island was brought to St. Andrews to build the town's first gallows. He had a reputation as a fine craftsman, and the people of St. Andrews wanted sturdy, reliable gallows should the need ever arise.

A consummate perfectionist when it came to his work, the contractor took to the task with energy and dedication. The structure was fine and sturdy, and Mr. Dunbar was pleased with the outcome. Everyone said it was one of the finest gallows they had ever seen. When he finished, Mr. Dunbar packed up his gear and returned home to Campobello Island. When he got home, he took the gold he had earned and put it in a little sack, which he then hid from his wife. He would need the money to pursue his personal interests.

Mr. Dunbar was known to have several bad habits, including spending the family money on gambling and alcohol, often leaving his wife to scrounge for household expenses. One night, shortly after her husband's return from St. Andrews (while he was out with his drinking buddies), Mrs. Dunbar went looking for the sack of gold. Following an exhaustive search, she found it where her husband had hidden it. She took the gold and buried it deep under the cover of darkness so that her husband would not find it and waste it.

When Mr. Dunbar returned later that night, he went to check his gold, only to discover it wasn't there. He was furious. Who would dare take the gold he had worked so hard to earn?

Storming up to his wife and confronting her with clenched fists, Mr. Dunbar demanded answers. "Where is my gold?" he barked. "I must have it returned at once," he bellowed.

Mrs. Dunbar, fearing the worst if her husband discovered where she had hidden the sack, refused to disclose its location. "I know not where your gold is," she insisted, although she suspected that her husband already knew she was responsible for taking it.

"I will give you one more chance," the angry Mr. Dunbar told his wife. "Tell me where the gold is."

Although fearful of her husband's anger, Mrs. Dunbar refused to tell her husband where the gold was, insisting that she did not know what he was talking about.

Try as she might to calm down her angry husband, Mrs. Dunbar subsequently fell victim to her husband's wrath. In a fit of anger, he killed his wife that night.

According to one local legend, Mr. Dunbar proceeded to cut up his dead wife and stuff her body parts into a pickle barrel which he hid under the floorboards of their Campobello home. Another story goes that he put her in the pickle barrel and then threw it over a cliff. Soon thereafter, it is said the body of Mrs. Dunbar washed up on a nearby beach.

No one knows which version is true. However, most agree that after disposing of his deceased wife, Mr. Dunbar then returned to the tavern and proceeded to brag to the other patrons about what he had just done. It seems Mr. Dunbar's drinking buddies were not impressed with his tale of murder and immediately sent for the soldiers. They came and returned him to the shire town of St. Andrews where the courts were. There, Mr. Dunbar was put on trial for the murder of his wife. The judge handed down a harsh punishment, sentencing Mr. Dunbar to be hanged until dead on the very same gallows that he had built with his own hands. And there Mr. Dunbar met his fate.

Today, it is said that the ghost of Mrs. Dunbar haunts Campobello Island. If you go to Dunbar Hill you will sometimes see the ghost of a woman with a lantern and a shovel, wandering aimlessly through the darkness. Local residents believe that is where she buried the sack full of gold. It remains hidden there to this day, attracting treasure hunters such as President Roosevelt, who was often seen on Dunbar Hill searching, some would say, for Dunbar's gold.

The Ghost of West Saint John

David Goss, a New Brunswick-based researcher and story-teller, has graciously agreed to share this story.

When the fishermen of Carleton-Old Saint John West saw gulls flying over the tidal rips of Hilyard's Reef across from their riverside fishing sheds, they knew the annual spring run of gaspereau were making their way upriver and soon their nets would be heavy with fresh spring fish.

Among those leaving their riverside homes at dawn on an April morning long ago was Daniel Keymore. Once into the water, he lifted his sail, caught the winds and was soon passing Navy Island, the wharves of Carleton, the old ferry dock, the Beacon light, and finally, past Partridge Island, around which most of the men fished.

That day, Daniel Keymore decided to travel further out into the bay. From his position near the Shag Rocks, he could see his home on the bluff behind Bay Shore. But that was soon to change when a storm suddenly blew up and Keymore's boat was swamped. He was drowned in the cold water of the Bay of Fundy.

The other fishermen returned to Carleton but Keymore's wife and children waited in vain for his return. On the morning after his drowning, his wife went out to the porch of their home, hoping against hope to see her husband miraculously appear on the shore. Instead she found only a huge codfish on her doorstep. Keymore never showed up nor was his body ever found.

One year later, on the anniversary of Daniel Keymore's death, his widow once again found a huge codfish on the porch of her home. For six years, every April 18, a huge codfish mysteriously appeared on the doorstep. On the seventh year, Mrs. Keymore remarried and moved her family to Carleton about one mile away. On the anniversary of Keymore's death, the house he and his wife had shared mysteriously burned to the ground. Firemen responding to the flames found only a pile of ashes with a huge codfish on the top.

The ghost of Daniel Keymore is still seen to this day by fishermen in Saint John West. Though his homestead is long gone, it has been reported that early in the morning of April 18, Keymore walks up from the docks near the Harbour Bridge toll plaza carrying a huge codfish over his back. He proceeds up King Street and then takes the hill up Prince to Tilton's Corner, where he makes a sharp left turn. Walking between the tombstones of the old Methodist cemetery, he heads towards his original home on the Bay Shore bluff, overlooking the spot where he drowned.

Those who try to follow Daniel Keymore usually lose him in the early morning mist, so no one has found a codfish near his old cottage recently. But that doesn't stop West Siders from keeping a sharp lookout for him every April 18.

The Legend of the Falling Trees

Port Royal in Annapolis Royal, Nova Scotia, is an important historical site because of its links to French-Canadian culture, commerce and colonization. It was also the site of important Mi'kmaq and French interaction from 1605 to 1613. The Canadian government rebuilt the Habitation at Port Royal in 1940 after much lobbying and research by several dedicated preservationists. Today, the Habitation not only commemorates historic events of the distant past, but serves as a landmark in Canada's preservation movement. According to local resident Jim Howe, who worked at the landmark throughout the 1950s and '60s, it is also a place where one can expect to find many unexplained phenomena.

"I had worked for many years at the Habitation in Port Royal," he says. "One day, as I was standing on one of the platforms that overlook the bay, I saw a taxi come into the gate. Usually taxis brought American tourists, but who should appear but an elderly native lady, a second younger lady and a small boy who was the son of the younger lady. They got out at the gate where I greeted them. That's when I recognized the woman as one of the Pauls, a local native family. I said, 'Madelyn, is that you?' She said, 'No, it's Christine.'"

Jim had remembered that the Pauls lived in the area and knew many of the children from those earlier days, but he had not seen them for many years.

"But I told her that I remembered her and her sister Rosie from when I was in Grade 3," Jim continues. "When I asked what had brought them to the Habitation, they told me they were on their way Delapse Bluff where they were going to cut black ash for the splints they needed for baskets.

One of the oldest settlements in North America, Port Royal has strong links to the unexplained.

The natives had done this for centuries. Delapse Bluff, where the French used to go to worship, was a prime spot for that sort of thing. I had been back there myself several times and knew the area where they were headed. It was still visible from the Habitation platforms."

Before they began their trek, Jim invited the party to tour the historic landmark. "They belonged here. Their people had been key to the settlement. I told Christine and the younger woman, her niece, that their ancestors had come to this spot and they were very supportive of the early settlers. The French colony would never have survived without the help of the native people. As I took them through the buildings of the settlement, the blacksmith shop and the fur room, I could see Christine was connecting with her past. I had never had more receptive visitors in my life. She was definitely connecting with her ancestors. She would put her hands on the walls and touch them as if to communicate with the past. She touched the furs and sat in the chairs. It was very moving and very spiritual."

Following the tour, the elderly lady and her family went off to the bluff in search of the black ash. For the next few days, Jim said, he often thought about them and wondered how they were doing in their quest.

"On the third day when I came to work, I was surprised to find Christine, her niece and the small boy crouching near the gate," he says. "When I asked them what was wrong, this was their explanation. They told me that the ash is selected by putting your ear against the trunk and tapping it. You can tell by the sound if there is an interception of knots or branches along the way that would destroy the straight grain needed for the baskets. The niece said they had made camp and settled in and everything seemed to be fine. Before they went down for the night, the niece said, they had gone out to the trees and tapped them to see what shape they were in. They planned to cut some trees in the morning."

However, sometime during the night, the three were awakened by a sound coming from the woods. "From the edge of the clearing, they heard, 'tap, tap, tap.' Despite their concern, they forced themselves to go back to sleep. The next night, they heard it again. This time, it was as if the trees were vibrating. In fact, the tapping was so powerful that they were frightened. They had never experienced anything like this in the past and Christine was well over 80 years of age. It was absolute terror for them."

The next day, the two women and the young boy returned to the Habitation where Jim found them. "The registration of terror was still on their faces. I remember it vividly."

Within a short while, a taxi came to take them away.

Later that fall, Jim says he heard that Christine had died.

What does all of this mean? Perhaps nothing, unless you believe in the old Mi'kmaq legends.

On the morning when he found them near the gate of the Habitation, Jim says that Christine knew she was going to die soon. "She told me the tapping they had heard the previous two nights was the old people. In the old legend, it goes that Glooscap shot arrows in the ash trees. As the trees split, out stepped a brave or a squaw. That was the creation of the native people, according to the legend. That morning Christine told me that the tapping was the old people calling to her, telling her that it was soon time for her come to them."

According to some stories, Jim says, such occurrences are related to the Legend of the Falling Trees. "When you hear a tree fall in the woods of its own volition, that's the symbol of death."

"She knew it," Jim says. "She knew the legend."

The Legend of Devil's Island

Near the mouth of Halifax Harbour is a small clump of land known locally as Devil's Island. Once inhabited by early German settlers, the island has long been deserted and the trees have all been felled. However, according to many local stories, at one time Devil's Island was the site of many strange phenomena.

Glenn Coolen has come to realize that many ghost stories and legends survive in areas once inhabited by German and Scottish settlers. That's why he isn't surprised by the legend of Devil's Island.

"It was said that numerous strange things happened way out there in the harbour. Today, there are no trees on the island, but at one time it was heavily treed and there used to be 13 families living there," Glenn begins. "Today, there are none. A number of years ago, it is said, one of the island's residents decided to have a party for all his neighbours and friends on the mainland and the island. In attendance was a young man by the name of Casper Henneberry. Casper was a common name in those times and Henneberry was the dominant family name at that time. The people of the island were fishermen."

Glenn says as far as he knows, the story takes place at the beginning of the 20th century.

"It is said that Casper came along to the party, arriving sometime during the day. Now it appears Casper was quite the drinker and had begun drinking immediately upon his arrival. Come suppertime, Casper was feeling pretty good and as nightfall came, Casper was pretty drunk. Come midnight, Casper could hardly stand up on his own two feet without assistance, but he did make his way out of the house at around midnight. He returned about an hour later, around one o'clock."

When Casper returned, he had his own story to tell.

"When he got back to the house, he threw open the door of the house where all of his friends who had gathered could see him. He was a mess. His colour was white and pale and he was wet."

His friends were concerned for Casper so they asked him, "Casper, what has happened to you? Where have you been? What's troubling you?"

As Casper related his tale, the others were astounded by what they heard.

"He told them that he had been down along the bank near the water for a brief spell. When he looked into the water he had seen a fish, a halibut in fact. Furthermore, he told them that this fish had started talking to him. He said he heard a voice coming from the fish and the fish had stated that he was the Dark Lord himself. That's right, Casper said, the fish had told him he was the Devil. The fish had also said it was going to take his life away from him in the next 24 hours and that it was going to snatch his soul away and drag it down to Hell."

Although his friends dismissed Casper's remarks as drunken ramblings, they could see that he was very upset.

"Whatever the case, on the very next day, Casper Henneberry was found in the middle of Halifax's Chebucto Harbour in his dory. He was quite dead. It is an interesting coincidence to be told one day you're going to die and then the next day to actually find yourself in that very predicament."

Had something strange or supernatural happened to Casper Henneberry? One is inclined to think so, considering the story that Casper had related only a few hours before his death.

"Casper's death could be blamed on a number of natural things—suicide or murder or inclement conditions or too much alcohol or exposure to the elements."

But there was no way the man could have drowned while sitting in his dory—or was there?

According to the legend, Glenn says, an immediate examination was conducted on Casper's remains. "When they found him, his dory was floating in the middle of the harbour. He was still sitting upwards in the dory and still clutching the oars, one in each hand as if he was rowing. It was the death grip, to be sure."

While no one considered the man's death a possible drowning under such circumstances, the entire community was shocked when it was confirmed that Casper had, indeed, died of drowning.

"Dories had high sides and although Casper remained in the seat and was clutching the oars, the medical exam revealed he had drowned. His body was contorted to such an extent and twisted to such a degree that his friends concluded that Casper had, in fact, been visited by the Devil and that the Dark Lord had claimed his life by snatching away his soul."

In honour of their friend's untimely death, the friends named the island Devil's Island.

Ox Tales

Thanks to Gary Selig, curator of the DesBrisay Museum in Bridgewater, Nova Scotia, we have the following explanation of the ox's mysterious place in Maritime folklore.

In a booklet entitled *The Ox in Nova Scotia*, Gary writes, "Before the arrival of machines, work that was too hard for a man to do was carried out with the help of trained animals. For thousands of years, the ox has helped do everything from cultivating crop land to moving buildings. The domestic steer, a castrated bull, is trained to become a working ox…The steer must then be trained to work before it is considered an ox.

"In rural areas, where the economy was underdeveloped and thrift was a way of life, oxen were cheap to feed, being able to graze most of the year and requiring a limited amount of grain. Their slow but steady power was easy on farm implements where sharp collisions with underground rock and stumps could damage equipment. Perhaps the most significant advantage over the horse was that when oxen were too old to be worked, they could be slaughtered and sold or eaten."

The ox plays an important role in many Maritime beliefs, particularly in rural Nova Scotia where tales of witchcraft and oxen are common. That is certainly the case in Lunenburg County.

In the same booklet, researchers record a story by Roger Doucet. "I could tell you a story I heard about witch work which we don't believe. This old gentleman…I would set alongside of him in the store and I did not tell him I did not believe. I was a young man then. I would have insulted the old gentleman.

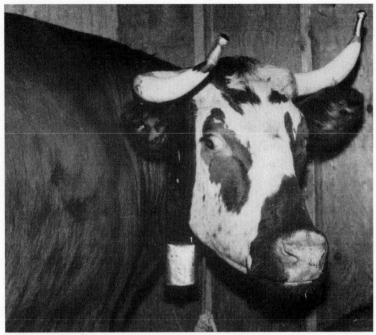

The ox holds a special place in rural Maritime folklore.

"He said this man had a load of something—I've forgotten what he said was on the wagon. And he had to go up this hill to go to his house and he went part way up the hill and could not go any further. The oxen couldn't haul the load. He said a man came along and told him to cut the eleventh spoke from the front wheel. He said, 'Your load'll go then.'

"The man cut out the spoke and soon as it was cut, he didn't have to tell the oxen to go. He said they just went. Took the load where he wanted it. I heard the old fellow say that."

John Kaulback shares a similar story.

"I'll never forget it. The nicest pair I think we ever had. My father left me back in the woods to come out on my own. He came out ahead. He had a horse, I guess with a load of wood and I had a load of pulpwood on with the oxen."

"There's an old chap that came out when he seen the oxen. He was talking to 'em, was brushing 'em all down, saying what fine oxen they were. Well, I went to haul the wood. They would not haul that out of his yard.

"They always said that old man was a witch. That's the only time I ever believed in witches. He must of put a spell on those oxen because they would not pull…for some reason or another."

Earle Veinotte tells another story.

"They'd trade oxen, you know. Lots of times you'd get a miserable pair, one would work and one wouldn't. I can remember years ago, I heard the old man talk about it. A fellow came over here from Oakland with his oxen with a load of grain on. He was going across to Mahone Bay. Somewhere down here on this side of Mahone Bay one ox got balky. He laid down and there he was.

"So the old fellow said, 'I'll take straw and set a fire under you. See if I can't get you up.'

"Well he did get him up. But he was a balky old ox, he only wanted to work so long. Then he just went ahead enough so that the wagon caught on fire. That ox hauled the wagon over the fire and the whole thing burned up. Fire went up through and burnt his wagon up. In order to save his oxen, he had to take them off of the pole and get 'em down and let his wagon burn up.

"That ox said to the man, 'You, you tried to burn me up. I'll burn your wagon up.'

"Yes sir, and that is just what happened."

The Ghost Ship of Beaver Harbour

Some of the greatest Maritime ghost stories come from legends passed down from one generation to the next. Based loosely on fact and actual events, some of these legends often take on lives of their own, growing and changing until they become more like fiction. Such is the case of the ghost ship that supposedly sails the icy waters of Beaver Harbour in New Brunswick.

Valerie Evans, a Saint John researcher and writer, says while she has never seen the ship herself, she has heard the stories of local people who claim they have seen a fiery ship sailing into the harbour. Concerned for the safety of those on board the crippled vessel, the villagers have been known to jump into their own boats and head toward the burning ship to help those in distress.

Only no matter how hard these people row, Valerie adds, they never draw any closer to the burning vessel.

"Some people, they've rowed and rowed for long periods of time, but they were never able to reach the ship. However, they apparently can hear the cries of those on board. 'Help me!' they scream. 'Help me!'"

Then suddenly the ship vanishes.

The question remains, was it ever really there in the first place?

Valerie says as far she knows, there is no historical record to verify that any ship ever burned in Beaver Harbour, but isn't that what makes this a mystery?

The Legend of Patty Bergan

Legend has it that deep in the centre of the old Loyalist Burial Ground in Saint John, New Brunswick, you will find the spirit of young Patty Bergan, perched high in the crook of an aging tree. He was hanged several hundred years ago for petty theft. It is also said that on some nights, if the wind is blowing just right, you will hear the young boy laughing.

Joan Helyar, who once operated a walking tour of the city called "Legends, Ghosts and Real-life Tales," says that according to the story, the young boy was 10 years old at the time of his death. It is said he was caught stealing a loaf of bread to eat. Theft in those days was a serious crime which young Patty paid for with his life. While the legend of Patty Bergan is popular in Saint John, there is some information that suggests portions of the story may not be entirely accurate.

Historical records show that an 18-year-old Patty Bergan was hanged by the neck for stealing 25 cents several centuries ago. Was that the same Patty Bergan? Joan agrees there is no way to clear up this discrepancy, but she doesn't see the value in trying to.

"It's a good ghost story," she says. "And it's part of the city's traditions, so it continues to be told."

Joan says she had a personal experience with the legend that left her a little edgy. "During one of my tours on an evening in July [2001] just as I was telling the group the legend of how, if you listen, you can hear Patty Bergan laughing, directly across from where we were standing a large black crow started calling. And you know, it left us all a little unnerved."

6

Maritime Mysteries

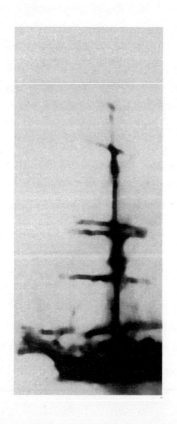

Don't Walk Behind Me

Marilyn Atwood, who lives on Nova Scotia's South Shore, tells the story of a strange phenomenon that she remembers from her childhood.

Back in the early 1930s, a shy young fisherman from one of the southernmost islands off the coast arrived at a small village store one day in a state of agitation. After several embarrassed false starts, he confessed that his wife had left him and gone off with another man.

After some hedging, he admitted he had no idea who the other fellow might be and that, in fact, he had never before laid eyes on the man.

"But if your wife has a boyfriend," the storekeeper said, "surely you must have some idea of who he is."

"Dempsey" insisted he had never seen the fellow. He told the storekeeper the strange man must have been calling on his wife, Myrtle, while he was at sea.

After some sympathy from those loafing about the store, the depressed young man made a few purchases and left. His tale surprised everyone. Myrtle had been a typical young fisherman's wife—plain of face and pleasant to meet, but never to anyone's knowledge making the least effort to attract a member of the opposite sex. Still, they had to admit that Dempsey was not exactly a prize catch as husbands went.

The gossip eventually died down, as it does in most small communities. In time, however, folks noticed that when Dempsey walked down the island road, he seemed nervous, constantly turning to look behind him. Moreover, he now came in bright daylight instead of at twilight as had been his previous custom. A fisherman mending his nets near that road said that as Dempsey passed him one day, he distinctly heard him muttering.

"Don't walk behind me!" the second fisherman heard Dempsey say, although there was nobody on the road but Dempsey himself.

Another neighbour, who had occasion to call at Dempsey's property one day, was shocked when he saw Dempsey approach the house, wait a moment and call out to the empty air, "Myrtle! Don't walk behind me!"

"He's going nuts," the neighbour later told the other island residents. "He's up there yelling at his wife and she was gone ages ago." But no one had seen or heard of Myrtle in many months. No one had any idea to where she could have possibly gone or with whom.

Apparently, no foul play was suspected in the case of Myrtle's disappearance. Dempsey was under no suspicion, since he was the meek and steely type. And so things carried on for some time.

Occasionally—although not any more often than he had to—Dempsey would go into town. By then he had stopped shaving. His beard was so wild that the teenagers said he was beginning to sprout brier bushes and birds' nests. He also walked almost crab-like in his effort to watch the street behind him. When someone followed closely behind him on a sidewalk, which was usually hard to avoid in a busy town on a Saturday afternoon, Dempsey would just about go berserk.

"Stop walking behind me!" he would scream, rolling his eyes like an angry billy goat.

Reclusive and eccentric, Dempsey became the laughing-stock of the town. But when he began to attack people who followed too closely behind him, the man's plight stopped being funny.

Finally committed to a mental hospital, Dempsey at first appeared quite sane. Then one day, as a red-haired nurse took Dempsey to the infirmary for x-rays, she let her patient get a bit ahead of her in the corridor. Dempsey landed on her like a tonne of bricks. His fists flailed. His feet stomped.

"Myrtle!" he screamed. "Don't walk behind me." It was said Myrtle also had carrot-coloured hair, so that may have caused Dempsey to lose his temper.

The nurse, accustomed to such unusual actions from the patients, took the attack in stride. She soon had Dempsey under control as a doctor rushed to her aid, quickly giving the distraught man a shot in the arm to quiet him down. Believing in the direct approach, the doctor asked the man straight out, "And where is Myrtle now?"

"Under the henhouse, damn her!" answered Dempsey, glassy-eyed as the effects of the drugs began to calm him down. "But the little witch won't stay there. Her ghost's been dogging my tracks just the way she always did...walked behind me everywhere I went—Dempsey do this, Dempsey do that—until I had enough of it. I just couldn't take it no more. Make her stop following me, doc, please."

The doctor promised he'd do his best. As far as we know, he kept his promise. His efforts were instrumental in getting Myrtle—or what was left of her—out from under the henhouse and into a proper corner of the local cemetery.

To this day, the story of Dempsey and the persistent ghost remains a mystery.

The Mystery of the Vanishing Crew

One of the greatest Maritime sea mysteries of all times began near Parrsboro, Nova Scotia, in December 1858 when the brigantine *Amazon* was built and launched. The vessel would become the subject of many tragic stories and in particular a tale that even to this day makes one's hair stand on end. Under its second name, *Mary Celeste*, the Nova Scotia-built vessel became synonymous with stories of ghost ships sailing the Atlantic Ocean.

According to Parrsboro teacher, historian and Maritime folklore collector Conrad Byers, the story begins with the ship's launching from Spencer's Island just outside of Parrsboro. A hard-luck ship almost from the start, the *Amazon*—built to carry lumber as her main cargo—ran into trouble during her maiden voyage. Within her first 24 hours at sea, the ship's captain died of a heart attack. The ship, Conrad points out, had not even left the bay. That, he adds, was only the beginning of her misfortunes. During her first trip to New Brunswick, she got tangled up in some fishing weirs and was extensively damaged. After that, she was loaded with lumber and sailed to England where she immediately ran into more trouble, becoming stuck in the English Channel.

Eventually, several years after her launch, the *Amazon* encountered a storm off the coast of Cape Breton Island and ran aground, again sustaining serious damage. The owners were forced to sell her, and subsequent owners fared no better than the previous ones. Finally, an American entrepreneur bought the *Amazon* in 1871 and repaired her.

The Mary Celeste *earned a place in Maritime folklore after her crew and passengers vanished without a trace in 1872.*

The vessel was renamed *Mary Celeste* and she was commissioned to carry barrels of industrial alcohol to Genoa, Italy.

On November 7, 1872, the *Mary Celeste* sailed out of New York Harbour carrying 1700 casks of raw alcohol. On board the vessel were the captain, Benjamin Spooner Briggs, his wife Sarah and their two-year-old daughter Sophia. The brigantine also had a crew of seven men on board.

These ten people were never seen or heard from again, resulting in one of the greatest seafaring mysteries of all time.

On December 4, 1872, the crew of another Nova Scotia-based brigantine, the *Dei Gratia*, spotted the *Mary Celeste* floating aimlessly near the Azores. The *Dei Gratia* crew boarded the vessel where they found signs (such as food preparation and a sheet of music on a small organ) that the ship had been quickly abandoned. They also found the lifeboat was missing but all the crew's belongings were still in their quarters, suggesting a hasty evacuation from the ship. The *Dei Gratia* boarding party also found that several of the casks were leaking their contents all over the hold.

Also of note was the final entry in Captain Briggs' log, which included the last recorded location of the *Mary Celeste*—378 miles from where it had been intercepted by the *Dei Gratia*. The *Mary Celeste* arrived in Gibraltar under its own sails on December 13, 1872, right beside the *Dei Gratia*. There, the mystery of the missing crew was thoroughly investigated. But after gathering evidence and testimony from the boarding party that had discovered the *Mary Celeste* and claimed the vessel as a derelict, a British board of inquiry concluded that piracy or foul play was unlikely. An extensive effort by authorities failed to determine the fate of the *Mary Celeste*'s crew.

Despite a search of the vessel, Captain Briggs, his family and the entire crew were never found. It appeared as though they had all vanished into thin air. Many theories and much speculation exist about what could have happened to the crew. Stories tell of alien abduction, attack by a giant man-eating octopus, an underwater earthquake whose force threw everyone into the sea, a bloody mutiny by the crew and even a raid by blood-thirsty pirates who threw the crew and passengers into the watery depths of the Atlantic.

There is one plausible theory, however, that seems to be widely accepted as an explanation for the lost souls on board the ill-fated *Mary Celeste*. It has been suggested that, despite his years of sailing experience, Captain Briggs had never carried crude alcohol on any of his ships. The change in temperature in a warmer climate may have caused the alcohol casks to leak. Fearing that the cargo might ignite and explode, Briggs may have ordered a hasty, but ill-conceived evacuation. That would explain the disappearance of the lifeboat. While it is believed that the crew had planned to return to the ship, it is possible that a wind may have blown her out of their reach, leaving the ten souls to float helplessly on the Atlantic Ocean. Or, it has been suggested, perhaps a huge wave may have come up and swamped the overcrowded lifeboat.

Despite the theories, the mystery that surrounds the disappearance of the *Mary Celeste*'s crew and passengers continues to intrigue and haunt the coastal communities of the Maritimes. But one thing is known for sure. After the disappearances, the *Mary Celeste* continued to sail for 12 more years, during which she was beset by collisions and fires. In that period, she was sold 17 times. Finally, in 1884, the *Mary Celeste* was bought by a captain who filled its hold with worthless cargo and ran her aground on Rochelois Reef near Haiti in an attempt to sink the jinxed ship and collect the insurance.

Defiant to the end, the vessel refused to go down without a fight. Eventually it was stripped by salvagers and then torched. The *Mary Celeste* sank to the ocean floor where it remains to this day, although its wreck was recently discovered by a group of Canadian sea adventurers.

Shadow Knows

A childless Maritime couple—a fisherman and his wife—lived in an old house near the ocean and kept two pet dogs. Shadow was a shaggy brown collie with a white tip on his tail. Ben was scarcely more than a pup, a lively little white terrier who trotted at the old dog's heels and seemed to be very fond of him.

When old Shadow died at the age of 15, little Ben was lonely and sad. He spent a part of each day searching for Shadow or lying on Shadow's old rug beside the fire.

The year following Shadow's death, the couple built a new bungalow near the old house and moved in, using the old house as a storage shed. Little Ben moved with them and seemed happier, spending no more time searching for his dead companion. The next year passed happily. Then, on the evening preceding the second anniversary of the old dog's death, the fisherman's wife got a surprise.

At first she did not realize that she was seeing anything unusual. She had crossed the yard and was about to enter the old house where they stored garden tools, firewood and other necessities. She saw something white bobbing along ahead of her in the starlight. Then the hunter's moon broke briefly from behind the clouds and revealed to her the figure of Shadow as he was trotting along ahead of her with the white tip of his tail bobbing as he moved. It was such a natural sight that she did not realize the unnaturalness of it. She absentmindedly assumed that old Shadow wanted back into the house to go to his bed in the corner. She held the door open and the dog passed inside exactly as he had done many times in the past.

But when the woman flipped on the light switch, she came to her senses. There was no dog. What's more, the sight of the deserted kitchen drove home the reality. She had seen Shadow. Surely it had been the familiar form of the old dog that until two years ago had trotted at her heels daily. But she knew it couldn't have been. Shadow was dead. Had she seen his ghost?

Her husband shook his head in disbelief when she told him of her strange experience.

"You were daydreaming," he told her. "Thoughts of Shadow must have been there in your mind whether you were aware of them or not. It'll be two years tomorrow since he died."

In the morning, Ben seemed restless. Sniffing and whining and trotting up and down the path, he disappeared finally into the woods behind the barn. It was the last time the couple were to see Ben alive, for he never returned.

They thought at first that their pet was off chasing rabbits and squirrels, so they didn't worry. Later they searched and called to no avail. At last, a neighbour came to tell them Ben had been found dead on a forest road—a road that his old pal Shadow had often followed during his lifetime. Ben had been killed instantly by a hunter's bullet.

They brought home the body of the little dog and buried it beside old Shadow in the front yard. "Because," said his mistress, "I'll always believe that Shadow came back to fetch him. Shadow knew that Ben's time was up and they would want to be together."

The Great Amherst Mystery

In what has been described as perhaps the greatest recorded case of poltergeist possession of all time, a young Nova Scotian woman was seemingly attacked and nearly driven mad by an unidentified and evil presence.

The year was 1878 and the place was Princess Street in Amherst, a small town in central Nova Scotia which sits near the New Brunswick border. Although he does not consider himself an expert in the Great Amherst Mystery, Charlie Rhindress, who operates the Live Bait Theatre in Sackville, New Brunswick, researched the case and wrote a play based on the story of 19-year-old Esther Cox. It was called *Guilty*.

Charlie says Esther's story has become the stuff of local legend, spawning at least two books as well as countless newspaper and magazine articles in the hundred years since the events occurred. And for good reason, he adds.

For the most part, people who claim to see ghosts report them to be benevolent, as if they were sent to deliver a message or to stake claim to a piece of property or a structure, such as a house or a bridge. Ghosts have also been known to appear around a significant event or date and, in many cases, they are but fleeting apparitions—there one minute and gone the next. Other spirits, however, are more evil and have sinister motives. They are destructive and hurtful to those they haunt. These ghosts are known as poltergeists. It is widely accepted in Amherst and beyond that a poltergeist caused young Esther Cox much pain and suffering.

Esther's mother had died when she was a young child. After her father remarried, he left Esther and her younger sister Jenny with their grandmother. When the grandmother died, both Esther and Jenny went to live with their older sister, Olive; Olive's husband, Daniel Teed; and their two children. Also living in the rented house in downtown Amherst was Daniel's brother, John Teed.

Esther, while relatively plain-looking, was a typical rural woman. Nothing seemed out of the ordinary with her until one night she went on a date with one of the town's young men. During the date, something dreadful happened. While it isn't exactly clear what actually occurred, it is widely speculated that Esther was attacked by the young man. Some stories even suggest that Esther was brutally raped by her attacker. Whatever the case, the date marked a turning point in Esther's life—a turning point to the dark side of the unexplained and the paranormal. Immediately upon returning home from the date, Esther's troubles began.

Esther was in great distress and a considerable amount of emotional, if not physical, pain. Since it was late and everyone was sleeping, Esther crawled into the bed that she shared with Jenny. She was really upset and crying hysterically as she told her younger sister about the attack. Suddenly, they felt something moving under the bed sheets. When they looked, they saw the shape of what they thought was a mouse. Quickly jumping out of bed, Esther and Jenny frantically searched for the suspected rodent—but they found nothing. Despite removing the covers and the mattress, they could find no mouse. They assumed they had frightened it away. Climbing back into bed, the young women eventually fell asleep.

However, there would be few restful nights in the Teed house during the months that followed. The strange phenomena had begun.

The next night, as Esther and Jenny settled down under the covers, they were disturbed by noises coming from a box stationed at the foot of their bed that contained several patchwork quilts and other pieces of fabric scraps. Getting out of bed, the two women lit their lantern and went to investigate the noises coming from the box. Suddenly, the box leapt into the air, coming to rest on its side in the centre of the room. Esther and Jenny screamed in horror at what they had just witnessed. The others in the house came running to see what was the matter. But by the time Olive and Daniel arrived, the box had quieted down. As the terrified young women tried to explain what they had seen, the others concluded that Esther and Jenny were either imagining things or were just fooling around.

Nothing, however, could be further from the truth, as the events of the third night would clearly demonstrate.

The next evening, Esther told the others she was not feeling well and decided to retire early for the night with a slight fever. At about ten o'clock that night, Esther leapt from her bed and stood screaming in the centre of the bedroom. She told Jenny that she didn't know what was happening to her, but she felt like she was on fire and that she was going to die. Alarmed for her sister's well-being, Jenny quickly lit the lantern and was horrified at what she saw as the light illuminated the room. By this time, Olive and Daniel, who had heard the commotion, came rushing into the girls' room. Together they carried Esther back to her bed and watched in utter disbelief and horror as Esther's skin swelled and stretched until, it is said, Esther was twice her normal size and her eyes appeared to bulge as if they were going to pop from her face. Burning up with fever, the young woman's colour turned a blood-red. All those in the room believed Esther was about to die. Crying out in pain as her skin stretched to the point of bursting, Esther withered in agony for quite some time. Suddenly, from beneath her bed, there came several loud, deafening bangs that caused the room to vibrate. Almost immediately, Esther's fever broke and the swelling subsided. Esther quickly fell into a deep sleep as the others were left wondering about what they had just seen.

Four nights later, the same terrifying events recurred. But after this attack, Jenny and others noticed fingerprints embedded in the wood where Esther had grabbed a chair.

Mystified and concerned for the well-being of Esther, the family brought in doctors to examine her. There were all kinds of theories, including demonic possession and the possibility that the young woman's body had acted like a magnet, attracting the power and creating an electrical field around herself (at the time, electricity was a relatively new invention).

One of the doctors who examined Esther Cox was a Dr. Carritte. He would later report that during his sessions with the young woman he had witnessed many unexplained phenomena. For instance, he claimed, at one point he watched in disbelief as Esther's pillow moved beneath her head, untouched by any hands. He also said he heard the loud bangs from under the bed, but could not explain where they originated. And, he said, he watched as the bed-clothes were thrown across the room as if hurled by some unseen entity. Then, Dr. Carritte said, he heard a strange scratching noise, like a metal tool scraping into plaster, and watched as letters nearly a foot high mysteriously etched themselves into the wall above Esther's bed. The words eventually spelled out a message: "Esther Cox You Are Mine To Kill." Then, suddenly, a clump of plaster tore off the wall, flew across the room and landed at his feet.

During subsequent visits to the Teed house, the doctor witnessed other unexplained phenomena, such as potatoes flying through the air. He continued to hear the deafening noises throughout the house, including the roof, but he could not locate their origins.

Years later, when talking and writing about the events surrounding Esther Cox, Dr. Carritte insisted that although at first he was skeptical, there was absolutely no way that Esther Cox or her family was perpetuating a hoax of any kind. Of course, since Esther's ailments were beyond explanation, the doctor could do nothing to help the troubled woman.

In the months that followed, the haunting continued, growing more destructive and dangerous. Unexplained fires erupted throughout the house. Knives and forks, thrown by some unseen entity, stuck into the woodwork. Lit matches miraculously materialized out of thin air and dropped into beds. Furniture moved about by itself, flipping over or slamming into walls. Pails of water placed on a table would boil over. Loud slaps were often heard, followed by the sudden appearance of red finger marks on Esther's face. Sewing pins appeared from nowhere and were jabbed into Esther's face. One time, a pocket knife was forcefully ripped from the hand of a neighbour and thrust into Esther's back.

Charlie says the attacks grew so severe that Esther began to tell the others that she could see the ghosts in the room and they would often tell her what they were going to do.

Concern for Esther's health and safety continued to grow in Amherst. Word of the mysterious phenomena spread across the continent. Stories of the poltergeist attacks began showing up in newspapers across Canada and in the United States, including New York and Boston. At this point, an actor, Walter Hubbell, who was part of a travelling theatre troupe that was touring Nova Scotia, showed up in Amherst intending to write a book exposing the great hoax of Esther Cox. Taking a room in the Teed house, he soon began witnessing firsthand the phenomena that had terrorized the young woman. He later wrote a book detailing the attacks and the strange occurrences at the house. It was called *The Great Amherst Mystery* and is considered the authoritative account of the phenomena that shocked so many people.

Walter Hubbell also took young Esther on tours throughout Nova Scotia and New Brunswick, thinking that people would pay to see the mysterious young woman who was possessed by such evil forces. Unfortunately, audiences were usually left disappointed, as the strange manifestations would not show themselves. "She'd sit on stage and Walter would explain what had happened," Charlie says. "Audiences showed up hoping they'd see it, but of course nothing happened. In some cases, audiences acted very badly and some actually chased them out of town."

As the attacks grew more dangerous, the landlord told the Teeds they could no longer keep Esther at the house because he feared she was going to burn it down. Olive and her husband sent Esther to live with friends of the family. Nothing would happen while she was away and after a while Esther would come home. But as soon as she was in the Teed house, the phenomena started once again. Esther eventually ended up living with a family on the outskirts of Amherst where she was to help look after the young children.

"But one day," Charlie says, "Esther came running out of the barn crying that the ghosts had told her they were going to set fire to the barn. And indeed, the barn burned to the ground, killing a bunch of livestock in the process."

Since the fire was suspicious, Esther was sent to jail on a charge of arson. She spent three months there, but it was in jail, of all places, that her fortunes actually took a turn for the better. She met a man from nearby Springhill and he came to visit her there. They became close friends and as soon as Esther was released from jail, the pair were married. The man also took Esther to see an Indian medicine man who, it is said, performed an exorcism.

After that, Esther and her new husband moved to Massachusetts and the ghosts miraculously disappeared. In 1912, Esther died at the age of 53 of natural causes, but she refused for the rest of her life to talk about what had happened to her in Amherst.

Today, the Great Amherst Mystery remains just that—a mystery.

7

Forerunners
and
Premonitions

Did You See That?

Do some people possess the special ability to foresee the future? Can they see when someone they love, perhaps a family member or a close friend, is going to face some sort of tragedy and maybe even death?

In the Maritimes, it is commonly believed that certain people do have such an ability. They are more likely to be in touch with their emotions, making them good candidates to see or hear forerunners. According to renowned Nova Scotia researcher Helen Creighton, forerunners are supernatural occurrences that announce a coming disaster. They may also be called tokens or visions, but throughout Nova Scotia (not to mention the other Maritime provinces) and among people of every descent, the popular name is forerunner. Occasionally, but only very rarely, forerunners foretell happy events, but more often than not they predict death.

Such is the case for the people in the following stories.

~

Dorothy from Truro, Nova Scotia, says she still gets goose bumps and cold chills when she thinks about the time she saw the forerunner of her first husband only minutes before she learned that he had just died.

It was July 1976, she recalls. "It was a hot day, a Friday. Me and my children were waiting for Jim to come home from work. We were all packed and were waiting for him to go camping. They were anxious and restless. It was hot and they wanted to get to the lake so they could get in the water. I've got to admit that I was looking forward to that myself."

Many Maritime tales of forerunners and premonitions are closely tied to fishing ports like this one on Nova Scotia's South Shore.

Jim should have been home between four o'clock and four thirty, depending upon the traffic conditions. If he had been late getting away from work, Dorothy knew he would have phoned because he wouldn't have left her alone to handle the kids without warning. By quarter to five, Dorothy says she was beginning to feel a little anxiety, since she knew it was not like Jim to be late, especially when they had prepared for a family outing.

"All of a sudden, I just had this terrible feeling in the pit of my stomach that something wasn't right," Dorothy says. "All I could think of was that something had happened to Jim. I couldn't shake the feeling. It was like a little voice inside telling me that Jim was in some kind of danger."

By five o'clock, Dorothy was beside herself and the children were starting to get to her. She knew if Jim didn't soon arrive or if she didn't soon hear from him, she'd go out of her mind. Maybe he had a flat tire or some other car trouble, she thought. Maybe he had been delayed at work and just couldn't get to a phone. Surely, he'd soon be home, she tried to reassure herself.

At ten minutes after five, almost an hour after Jim's scheduled arrival, Dorothy says she breathed a deep sigh of relief. Although she thought it odd, while sitting on the front steps she spotted Jim making his way down the sidewalk toward their home. He must have had car trouble and decided to walk home instead of phoning, she thought. Everything was as it should be, she assumed. They may be a few hours later in getting away, but Jim would get the car fixed and then they'd be off.

With anticipation and relief Dorothy watched her husband cross the street, walk up to the front gate and then, right before her eyes, vanish. "I know he was there," she insists, the emotions in her voice still conveying the desperation of the moment. "I know what I saw and no one will ever convince me otherwise. They can try to tell me it was stress induced or that I only thought I saw him, but he was there. I know it."

Quickly jumping to her feet, Dorothy made her way to the front gate and looked for Jim, but he was nowhere to be seen. "That's when it hit me," she says. "That's when I knew he was gone and that I had seen his forerunner."

Returning to the house, Dorothy waited quietly for the news that she knew would come. About half an hour later, police arrived on her front step with the devastating news that her husband had died in a car accident about three kilometres from home. An autopsy later revealed that Jim had suffered a massive heart attack while driving home that afternoon. He was dead before his car left the road. "We never knew he had a heart condition, but I knew he had died that day. I knew long before they ever came and told me."

~

Martha, who lives in a small community just outside of Yarmouth, Nova Scotia, shares a similar story. She believes her fisherman husband reached out to her one stormy night just before he died.

"It was a bad night, raining hard and the wind was blowing a gale. I knew it was going to happen," she begins. "I grew up around these parts. I heard the stories of women seeing their men before they died. I guess that's pretty common in places where they fish. We're used to the boats going down and sometimes you'd lose a handful of the local men all at one time. That happens a lot around here."

But, Martha says, "no matter how many times you hear about it happening some place else, you never think it will happen to you. You just never think that you'll lose someone close to you. But I guess we should know better. We should know that when the sea wants someone, there's no denying it."

It was a stormy night in January, she remembers. "All the fishermen knew that any boat out in that storm would be in trouble. They said the ice would build up and it would be hard to keep the boat afloat."

Martha's husband, Tommy, was out with three other men and she was worried for their safety. "I just wished they were home, but it wasn't meant to be. At about 10:30, while I was sitting in the living room watching TV and trying to keep my mind off the storm, I looked up and saw Tommy walk from the kitchen to the bedroom down the little hallway that leads from the living room. I was scared. I knew they hadn't come in. Tommy would have called me to come get him if they had come in."

Martha and Tommy had been married for only three years but she knew the routine. If the boat were ever to arrive at port outside of a scheduled landing time, he would call—no matter what time—for her to come pick him up.

"When I saw Tommy I just started crying. I knew he was gone. I knew I had just seen his forerunner."

The next morning, Martha received the devastating news. Tommy had been lost overboard when he was hit by a huge wave and lost his footing on the ice-covered deck. His body was never recovered.

~

From the Bathurst, New Brunswick, area comes a similar story of death and foreboding, but with a twist. Margaret now lives in Saint John, but she says when she was a youngster some 50 years ago, she saw the ghostly image of her grandfather's dog and she knew that her beloved grandfather had died.

"My grandfather lived alone after Grammy died," she begins. "But he kept Old Black around for company. He was a big, friendly mix-breed who loved us kids. They were always together. Grampy didn't go anywhere without bringing Old Black with him. They were good friends and he needed that."

Margaret recalls that she and the other children would often visit their grandfather and he would tell them stories of life on the sea and about the traditions of the old country. She enjoyed the stories very much and was always particularly interested in stories of the supernatural and ghosts. "He would tell me that's because I had the gift.

I don't know about that, but I think he would say that's the reason I knew he was dead long before anyone told me."

When she was 14, as she was walking along the beach one warm morning in September, she saw Old Black running down the beach toward her. As he got closer, she expected to see her grandfather come into sight, since "Old Black didn't go anywhere without my Grampy." The old man was in his eighties but still moved around quite easily, she recalls. He was very active for his age and often walked the beach with Old Black, so it was customary to see him there.

"I looked for him, but couldn't see him anywhere. But there was Old Black, just as plain as day."

Thinking Old Black wanted her to play, she raced toward the dog. But as she drew near him, Margaret says, "he just vanished. Just like that. He was there was one minute, gone the next. Obviously there was no explanation, but he was there. No one could ever convince me otherwise."

Heading home, Margaret, who had paid particular attention to her grandfather's tales of the supernatural, says she couldn't shake the feeling that something terrible had happened to her grandfather. When she finally reached home, her mother told her the devastating news. There had been a fire at her grandfather's home some time during the previous night and he couldn't get out. While there hadn't been a lot of fire damage, there was a lot of smoke and the old man had died of smoke inhalation.

Margaret was devastated. She had loved her grandfather very dearly. After the initial shock wore off, her thoughts turned to Old Black. What would happen to the dog? she wondered. Could they bring him home and look after him? She insisted her grandfather would want that. He would want someone to give Old Black a good home. He needed someone to love him.

Her mother quickly explained that Old Black had died as well. When firefighters found her grandfather's body in bed, they found the dog's body lying on the floor beside the bed. They assumed the dog had died of smoke inhalation as well.

It was some time before Margaret finally told her mother about what she had seen that morning on the beach. Her mother explained that she believed Margaret's grandfather and Old Black wanted to let her know that they were all right, that they hadn't suffered any pain.

"And I believe that. I really believe that Old Black was sent to me as a message," Margaret says. "I missed my grandfather and Old Black after that, but I took some comfort in the fact that I knew they were together and they were okay."

~

From the Eastern Shore of Nova Scotia comes the story of a woman who came face to face with her father only minutes before she learned he had died hundreds of miles away in Newfoundland.

Diane insists she had been going about her regular routine one night, not really dwelling on the fact that her father was on his deathbed over in Newfoundland. He had been diagnosed with cancer seven months earlier and his end was near. When she had been home to see him about a month earlier, she could tell he was in a great deal of pain and that the cancer was progressing quickly.

As Diane went about washing the supper dishes, she casually glanced out the kitchen window that provided her with a view of the backyard and, off in the distance, the Atlantic Ocean. As she stared off in the distance, her mind wandered to no place in particular and she lost track of what she was doing. Suddenly, Diane says, "There he was. With no warning at all, my father was standing there in my backyard. I could see him clearly. I could make out his face and he smiled at me. He didn't look like he was in any pain."

Diane says the vision lasted only a minute or two, then it was gone. "But he was there. I called my husband to come quick and take a look. He came, but he told me I was crazy, that it was just my mind playing tricks on me. He said I only thought I had seen him because I was worrying about him. But, honestly, I wasn't even thinking about him or home at that particular minute."

As Diane continued to insist that her father had been in their backyard, the phone rang. Diane would not answer it. "I told my husband to answer because I knew what it was. I knew it was my mother calling to tell me Dad had died."

Still skeptical, Diane's husband answered the phone and listened as her mother delivered the news. Diane's father had died about 15 minutes before.

~

In a small fishing village not far from Bridgewater, Nova Scotia, a mother still speaks of the night she saw her son only hours before she received the news that he had died in a fishing boat tragedy. It was late fall and Bertha explains that she and her husband, a retired fisherman who understood the perils of the fishing world, had just gone to bed. The time was around nine thirty.

Bertha says it was probably about 15 minutes after they turned in that night that she heard someone in the kitchen. Since all their children were grown up and either living with their own families or away working, she feared that they had an intruder. Shaking her husband awake, she insisted that they should call for help. Instead, he slid out of bed and made his way down to the kitchen to see who was there. Bertha remained in bed with the covers pulled up to her chin, awaiting her husband's return.

"I was afraid something was going to happen to him," she recalls. "He was an old man and if someone had broken in, he wouldn't be any match for them. I feared he would be hurt or killed."

Several minutes after her husband left the bedroom, Bertha heard footsteps coming up the stairs and down the hallway toward her bedroom. She first thought it was her husband returning, then she feared that maybe it might be the intruder coming for her. She was terrified as she saw the figure of a man come into the doorway and stop there. It was dark, but Bertha says she could tell it wasn't her husband, nor did she believe it was a stranger. As her eyes slowly adjusted to the darkness, she could clearly make out that the figure in the doorway was none other than that of her middle son Alex.

Bertha screamed. The figure disappeared and her husband rushed into the room. She was hysterical. Relating what she had just seen, she feared the worse. Having lived near the Atlantic Ocean all their lives, the elderly couple knew that this was a sign. They feared their son Alex was lost.

The next day, as news reports told of a sinking just off the coast of Nova Scotia, Bertha says they knew it was Alex's boat. Later that day, they learned the devastating news that their son had been lost at sea along with the other crew members.

"It was the worst day of my life," Bertha says. "It was terrible seeing Alex there in the doorway because I knew what it meant. I knew it was Alex because when he was a teenager and still living at home, every night after he came home and we were in bed, he'd stop and stand in our bedroom doorway for a few minutes. He wanted to tell us he was home. Sometimes, he'd stay and talk for a while. It may have been dark that night, but I know the figure in the doorway that night was Alex. I knew it and my husband believed me when I told him. We didn't want Alex to go fishing but he said he had to; he said it was in his blood."

~

Stories of forerunners and other visions are common throughout the Maritimes. Perhaps it's the traditions from the "old country," as some local residents explain it, but most Maritimers know when they see or hear something unusual it might just be more than mind games. It could be a message or a warning and most Maritimers take it to heart.

Riding With Father

Gordon Hansford of Kentville, Nova Scotia, freely admits that he believes there are things in this world that defy explanation. And maybe, just maybe, he says, ghosts are among those phenomena that we will never understand.

Gordon says there are times when things seem strange or have no explanation, when in fact the simplest explanation exists. He recalls when he was a young man living in nearby Wolfville in 1940. He worked at the train station. There was a young lady living not too far from the station. Also nearby was the old Baptist burial ground.

The young woman lived in an upstairs apartment and could see the neighbourhood from that vantage point.

"One clear winter night following a light dusting of snow, the young woman looked out over the old burial ground and onto Main Street. It was then she saw someone coming through the graveyard. That was unusual, she thought. No one would be in there at this hour, so she watched the figure and she expected to hear the big iron gates as they squeaked when they were opened. But to her surprise, the gates did not open. Instead, the figure just vanished. It was midnight, so she became convinced that something unusual had just happened."

Gordon says the young woman was distraught. Naturally believing she had seen a ghost, she told her father. He promised that in order to ease his daughter's fears, the next night he would watch with her. There must be some reasonable explanation, he was certain.

"Sure enough, as they looked together the next night, it happened again. Like the previous night, the apparition came through the graveyard and then just disappeared."

It seems the story of the vanishing ghost in the Baptist cemetery went on to become something of a local legend. Gordon says he heard it many times, but he did not grasp its meaning until many years later when he overheard the woman, now much older, telling stories of the time she saw the ghost in the graveyard on Main Street.

After listening intently, Gordon says with a chuckle, "I realized this woman had not seen a ghost after all. I had worked at the station and after the midnight train had come and gone, I was done for the night. I used to travel home through the back of the graveyard. I went through the grave-yard, but instead of using the gate, I would squeeze through a small hole in the gate because it was such a noisy thing."

Gordon says he wasn't sure if he wanted to ruin the woman's story after all those years, but he finally told her the truth and she found it amusing. "So you see, some ghost stories have an explanation—but some do not."

For a man who likes to tell it like it is, Gordon says without hesitation, "Some things have happened in my life that have made me think there's another world that we don't know much about."

One of those things, he recalls, happened in 1966 while he was driving from Nova Scotia to the West Coast.

"I was driving all by myself and it can be a lonely trip. Sometimes when you're alone on big trip like that, you find yourself dozing off."

Gordon says he had passed through Lake of the Woods when it happened. Since the highway was just recently completed, there were no white lines yet to mark the way. It was a wet, dark night and the driving was difficult. "It was raining and there was no moon. You couldn't see very well. I really should have pulled off and had a rest."

Although he admits he had felt himself slipping into sleep, he pushed on, hoping to cover some highway with the decreased traffic. But he couldn't fight the exhaustion. Suddenly he fell asleep.

"Just like that, I was asleep. It can happen fast under those kinds of conditions."

Gordon doesn't know how long he was asleep behind the wheel, but he is certain that if had remained asleep much longer, his car would have left the road. "God knows what might have happened then. I might have been hurt or even killed."

But it wasn't meant to be.

"I swear that even though I was alone in the car that night, my father spoke to me and woke me up. He said 'Gordon.' That's all he said, but I know it was him. I recognized the voice as his. I have no doubt about that. It was him."

All of a sudden, as if shaken to consciousness, Gordon awoke. "For a minute, I didn't even know where I was. I immediately pulled off the road and got out of the car, walked around and stamped my feet until I got my head clear. Then I looked in the car to see who was in there. I needed to see whose voice I had heard, although I'm convinced that I heard my father's voice just as clear as a bell."

Over the years, as he's thought of the incident and told others about it, Gordon becomes more and more certain that his father woke him up that night and, in fact, may have actually saved his life.

"I know it was him. He was there with me that night."

Gordon admits the story may seem unlikely because, you see, his father had died in 1964—two years before Gordon's near accident.

Edward's Vision

The following story was first related in the *Bulletin* of Bridgewater, Nova Scotia, dated July 28, 1903.

Captain Diggdon, of the Nova Scotia schooner *Gold Seeker*, which was lost on the night of June 1 on the Mosquito Coast, arrived in New York City on Tuesday, July 21, on board the steamship *Yucatan*. Captain Diggdon tells an interesting story about the sinking of the *Gold Seeker*. The vessel was bound from South America for the Isle of Pines to take on a load of coconuts.

On the night of the wreck at about eleven o'clock, when the schooner was within ten miles of the Isle of Pines, Captain Diggdon retired to his cabin. He expected to reach his destination by daylight the following morning. But he could not sleep. A presentiment of trouble made him restless and he decided to return to the deck. Five minutes after he emerged from his cabin a sudden squall from the southeast struck the schooner. Its force was so great that the vessel was tossed around and then it capsized. In rolling over it imprisoned all on board except the captain and three sailors who were on deck at the time. Among those who were sleeping at the time and were lost were a Columbian custom-house officer, the ship's mate, the cook and the boatswain. It was reported that ten men were lost that night. Even if these men had been awakened by the incoming waters, they could have done nothing to help themselves.

On finding himself free from the wreck of the schooner, Captain Diggdon supported himself by clinging to floating wreckage. The three sailors saved themselves in the same manner, and when the squall had passed, the four succeeded in clearing the vessel's boat and making the Isle of Pines without additional hardships.

For Wilfred Fralic of Upper LaHave, on Nova Scotia's South Shore, the *Gold Seeker* tragedy holds special meaning, for one of those who perished was his grandfather, George Arthur Fralic from Mersey Point, a small fishing port on the outskirts of Liverpool.

Because he grew up in Nova Scotia and eventually made his living at sea, Wilfred is familiar with the tragic lifestyle shared by those who live along the rugged Atlantic coastline. Although the *Gold Seeker* went down 18 years before Wilfred was born, its story has intrigued and haunted him for most of his life. Not only did the tragedy represent lost lives; it also brought folklore to life that many people considered unbelievable.

Wilfred tells the tale as he remembers having it told to him.

On the night of June 1, 1903, Wilfred's great uncle, Edward Fralic (George's brother), was asleep in his Florida home. According to the story that Wilfred remembers, it was late at night, around eleven o'clock, when Edward became aware that something or someone was in his bedroom. The feeling was so intense that it awoke him from a deep sleep. Coming to his senses, Edward was alarmed to find a wispy vision of his brother hovering near his bed.

"What are you doing here?" Edward asked of George. Using the Maritime phrase meaning out to sea, Edward added, "I thought you were out on a trip." Although the presence did not respond, Edward became frightened as he immediately realized that he was seeing a forerunner of his brother. That usually spelled disaster and death.

According to the story Wilfred remembers, the vision lasted for only a few minutes before it vanished, but not before leaving a sense of foreboding and deep loss with Edward. He knew his brother was at sea and concluded that he was dead.

As news of the tragedy at sea spread, Edward kept the story of his strange visitor to himself. A week or so later, when family members in Nova Scotia finally called Edward to tell him that his brother had been lost at sea, he replied that he had already received word through a special messenger.

Over the years, Wilfred says, the story has given him goose bumps. It could be his Maritime upbringing or his own inexplicable experiences, but he insists that he believes in such things. "I certainly believe that this stuff happens. Why can't it?"

Was Edward Fralic having a nightmare on the night of June 1, 1903? Or did he have an unannounced visit from his brother who was drowning at sea? If so, what was the meaning of the visit? Wilfred says that over the years the family told themselves that George paid a visit to Edward that night to tell his brother that he was okay, that everything would be all right.

Who can really say for sure?

A Visitor From Beyond

Can people send their spirits over great distances to deliver messages to close friends or family members about impending death?

Some people believe they can.

Donna Maquire, who lives in Peggy's Cove on Nova Scotia's South Shore, says without hesitation she is a believer. She begins her story by saying, "I've told very few people about this because it's very bizarre, but it's true."

She explains: "Some 20 years ago, I had a very close friend. He was almost like a father figure to me. I knew his wife and daughters very well. His name was Ross and we were all very close."

Ross had been a naval commander all his life, but cancer had taken its toll on him. Donna says it was devastating to watch what the dreadful disease had done to the once-vital human being, but he still put up a brave fight for several years. The end finally came one summer night while Donna and her family had been away on Prince Edward Island. Donna says she has always felt terrible about not being there for him at the end, but she knows he was okay with that—because he told her so on the night he died.

"When we arrived at our destination on Prince Edward Island, there was a message from Ross' daughter telling us that Ross had died. I was terribly upset. I felt I should be home. I couldn't handle it; I went right to bed."

Although very emotional and distraught, Donna says with some conviction that she knows what happened next was real, that it was not a dream nor was it induced by grief for her dead friend.

"I had been crying pretty hard but I know, without a doubt, that Ross walked into that bedroom in that cottage on Prince Edward Island and looked directly at me. It was him. There was no doubt. He had bushy white eyebrows and piercing blue eyes. He looked very happy."

Donna says she was stunned by his sudden appearance but she was not frightened, even when Ross spoke to her.

"Donna," he said, "everything is fine with me. I don't want you to worry and I don't want you to disrupt your family vacation. You need this. There's nothing you can do."

Then he quickly disappeared.

Donna admits that to some people these things are impossible to believe, "But I know what happened. I know it was real."

Shiver Me Timbers

Conrad Byers of Parrsboro, Nova Scotia, agrees that many Maritime stories of ghost ships and other such mysteries have been embellished over the years—twisted and pulled with each telling to make them more exciting and suspenseful. However, he points out, a story involving a Captain Hatfield who sailed on ships out of Parrsboro during the 1880s and 1890s appears to be factual, thus raising many questions about the world of paranormal experiences.

"I knew Captain Hatfield's granddaughter," Conrad begins. "He was a religious and no-nonsense person. According to her, each time he told the story, he related it with such conviction and attention to detail, that everyone who heard the tale agreed that it must be true. Furthermore, it appears that no matter how many times the captain told the story, the details remained constant—another indication that whatever happened to Captain Hatfield out there on the Atlantic had left its mark."

On a return trip from the West Indies, Captain Hatfield's ship encountered a stretch of bad weather that lasted for several days. The crew remained awake for days as they fought desperately to keep the ship from foundering. With their knowledge and experience, the captain and his men kept the ship afloat and, miraculously, on course. When the storm died down, the entire crew was in need of rest. All but a few were relieved of their duties so that they could get some much-needed sleep. Before retiring to his cabin, Captain Hatfield gave specific instructions to the helmsman and mate, ordering them to stay on a certain course. He told the mate that he was going to his cabin to get some sleep and did not wish to be disturbed unless it was an emergency.

With that, Captain Hatfield made his way to his quarters where he settled down for a well-deserved rest. Feeling comfortable that his vessel was in good hands, the captain quickly drifted off to sleep.

No sooner had Captain Hatfield fallen asleep that somebody tapped him on the shoulder and told him to change course. The captain was furious. There had better be a good reason for his men to disturb him after he gave specific orders to the contrary. Angry as he left his cabin, Captain Hatfield intended to take this up with the mate. How dare he wake him up to tell him to change course when his orders had been clear?

Storming onto the deck, Captain Hatfield confronted the mate and the helmsman who appeared surprised to see the angry captain there; they thought he was fast asleep in his quarters. After Hatfied confronted the men with his anger, both the mate and the helmsman insisted that neither of them had gone to his cabin or awakened the captain. They also told Captain Hatfield that they were certain that none of the other crew had disturbed him and that they were still on the same course as per his orders.

Unsure of what to believe, Captain Hatfield left the deck and returned to his quarters. Again, after he had fallen asleep, he was awakened by someone with an urgent request that he order the ship to take a different course. Angry that someone in his crew was disobeying his direct orders, the captain returned to the deck several times. Each time, his men told him the same thing—no one had been to his quarters and the ship was still on the same course he had ordered.

Captain Hatfield was mystified. He knew and trusted his crew. If the mate said no one had disturbed him, then he was confident that was the case. But if none of the crew had awakened him, then who?

Puzzled, the captain returned again to his quarters. Despite his anger, exhaustion allowed him to drift off to sleep yet again. Within minutes, however, the alarm was repeated. Someone was shaking him awake and insisting that he change course.

Quickly opening his eyes, Captain Hatfield was able to catch a glimpse of the man who had just wakened him. Armed with the description, the captain had the entire ship searched. He felt there must be a stowaway on board and the man must be found.

The crew searched for quite some time, but could not find anyone. Captain Hatfield thought the entire ordeal was quite odd. He had been awakened several times and he knew he had seen a man exiting his cabin. While not necessarily a superstitious man, the captain began to wonder if this strange series of events was a sign of some sort. He became frightened. Perhaps there was danger ahead on their current course and this was a warning.

Unable to explain the strange occurrences on his ship, Captain Hatfield ordered the helmsman to take a new course, the one that had been ordered by the strange man in his cabin. Skeptical but confident that their captain knew what he was doing, the crew followed orders. Ten hours later, the lookout on Captain Hatfield's ship reported that he had spotted a lighthouse.

Impossible, the captain thought, since their new course was taking his ship farther out to sea. He asked the lookout if he was sure it was a lighthouse; the man replied in the affirmative.

Still unsure of what he would find, Captain Hatfield ordered the helmsman to head toward what appeared to be a lighthouse. However, as the ship approached its destination, they discovered that it wasn't a lighthouse after all, but instead a light belonging to an American ship in distress. On board the crippled ship, they found the crew was still alive but in a very bad way. Quickly bringing the crew on board his ship, Captain Hatfield and his crew watched in amazement as the other vessel sank out of sight. They had arrived just in time to divert a terrible tragedy at sea.

The captain of the second vessel, Captain Hansberry, reported that they had been adrift for several weeks after losing their rigging and being blown off course by a terrible storm. After floating helplessly from the normal shipping routes for several weeks, the entire crew accepted that they would not survive. They had given up all hope of encountering another ship in that area.

Which raised the question: what had brought Captain Hatfield and his crew to their location?

Accompanying Captain Hansberry on the ship was his wife. As she listened to Captain Hatfield's story of his being awakened and instructed to take an alternate course, she asked him to describe the man he had seen exiting his cabin.

Amazingly, she told Captain Hatfield that he had just given a perfect description of her father. He had also been a sea captain who loved to sail the waters of the Atlantic Ocean. But what was even more amazing, she said, was that her father had been lost somewhere off the Atlantic coast three years earlier.

For rescuing the American crew, Captain Hatfield received a presidential medal of honour, although he was quick to point out that the miraculous rescue would not have happened if it hadn't been for the stranger in his cabin.

A Messenger of Death

Fort Anne in the town of Annapolis Royal played a major role in European affairs in Acadia and Nova Scotia during the 17th and 18th centuries. The fort served as the seat of government and as a focal point of French and British settlement in the region. It was also the scene of numerous battles as the European powers fought for control of North America. Early in the 20th century, local residents campaigned to have the site's ruins preserved and maintained for future generations. Fort Anne became Canada's first administered national historic site in 1917.

Historian and local resident Jim Howe points out that Fort Anne has also been the site of many paranormal phenomena—including one he experienced.

"I think Fort Anne is an area where anything related to death can happen," he says. "The ground is just permeated with the blood of those who have been buried there. They would have been wounded, dismembered, neglected and everything else. It has been said that a truly historic site really exudes the past and you can say that about Fort Anne. There is a certain sense of foreboding there or a power or a loneliness that you can feel. It's almost as if there is a presence on the property."

Jim explains that he experienced that presence firsthand.

"It occurred in an area where I had heard other reports of strange things happening," he begins. "That may be significant, I suppose, but I really can't say for sure. Perhaps it is merely a coincidence; perhaps not."

Jim's experience involved a childhood friend with whom he had grown up and spent much time together. Although his buddy moved to Ontario, he says, the two remained very

Fort Anne in Annapolis Royal, where Jim Howe experienced a premonition of his friend's death.

close friends. "We grew up together in Annapolis. We went to school together and we saw a great deal of each other."

About 15 years ago, Jim says his friend developed terminal cancer. "That produced a significant change in him. Physically, he aged very quickly. You could see the cancer was progressing rapidly. It was really a great concern for me to see this happening to him."

One day, Jim recalls, he had left his office at Fort Anne to go into town to run an errand. "I can't really remember what I was going for, but I can recall very vividly what I saw. As I was heading toward the covered way (a dyke-like structure built to protect the soldiers during battle), I saw a figure coming over the covered way in my direction."

At first, Jim said, he thought it was a visitor, but then quickly realized what he was seeing.

"I immediately recognized the stance and the height. Everything was recognizable—everything except the face. I don't remember that at all. I knew it was my friend, but we weren't expecting him. He was supposed to be in Ontario. It wouldn't be unlike him to just show up unannounced, but in his condition I didn't think that would be too likely."

Regardless, Jim said he knew for sure that the figure he was seeing was that of his lifelong friend.

"I quickened my pace, anxious to see him. But as I came up to greet him, he just vanished. I tell you, there was no one there. My recognition of him had been quite full and complete. I knew my friend had been there only seconds earlier. I must say that I was quite perplexed by the whole thing."

Knowing that his friend was quite ill, Jim assumed that what he had just seen was a messenger announcing that his friend was near death. He was very upset by the ordeal.

"As I left the grounds of the fort, I crossed over the street. There I met my friend's uncle who was 92 years of age. The uncle greeted me with the news that my friend's cancer had progressed to the late stages. He said they were just waiting for the news."

Within a few weeks, Jim says, he received word from Ontario that his friend had lost his battle with cancer.

"I'm convinced that what I saw that day was a forerunner of some sort," he says. "I think it was telling me that I would never see my friend alive again. I knew it right away because I had a sad feeling about me after that. There certainly was an overwhelming sense of foreboding and worry. It was a messenger of death, to be sure."

Jim says he doesn't believe it was a coincidence that he saw the forerunner at Fort Anne. "When we were children we often played there. And a place like Fort Anne is very historic, with deep connections to death. I think it was a perfectly natural location for it to happen."

Signs, Signs,
Everywhere the Signs

Cape Breton Island was settled mostly by Scottish and French immigrants who were impressed by the area's strong resemblance to their homelands. Rugged and untamed, the island offers a unique blend of rocky coastline, mountains, valleys, rivers and lakes. The massive highlands in the northern reaches of the island represent the highest elevations in the Atlantic region.

Cape Breton's strong Scottish heritage is still evident everywhere. Gaelic is still spoken in some of the small communities nestled along the rugged coastline, and bagpipes and fiddles can often be heard, as the musical traditions have been passed down from one generation to the next. And just as Cape Bretoners' love of music and the *ceilidh* (a Gaelic word meaning party or gathering) runs deep, so does their belief in the supernatural.

Tourist promotions sing the praises of beautiful Baddeck. Nestled quaintly on the shores of the Bras d'Or Lakes, Baddeck was once home to Alexander Graham Bell, the famous inventor and teacher. It is now the home of "Sandra," who possesses special and unique qualities that occasionally cause great grief.

Such was the case many years ago when she foresaw the untimely death of her younger brother. Remembering the incident, Sandra points out that all of the women on her mother's side of the family are said to have certain skills. "They called it the sense or the power or the gift or the art or the curse—take your pick. But no matter what you call it, what they were saying was that we could see things before

Scenic Cape Breton Island is steeped in mysteries that defy explanation.

they happened. For me, I was aware that I had this extra sense from as far back as I can remember. Years later, I found out that my mother had it and so did my sister and our grandmother; my mother even said that my great-grandmother had it."

Today, Sandra talks openly about her gift but there was a time when it terrified her. "I had a terrible time with it when I was a child. It's an awful thing to see when something bad is going to happen. I don't know why it is with me that all I seem to see are the bad things. My sister sees a mixture of good and bad. Sometimes I think that would be nice. But I guess you have no control over that."

The family gift manifests itself in many different ways, Sandra explains. "It could be something subtle, like a feeling or an image that might flash in your mind. Or it could sometimes be something more like a dream or a vision, which is kind of like a dream with your eyes open."

Over the years, Sandra says she has seen a variety of things before they've occurred. "One time, I saw that my father was going to fall down into the cellar—and he did.

He wasn't badly hurt, but it scared me nonetheless. Another time, I saw a terrible two-car accident that left three people dead. And it happened just like I saw it. I've also seen storms before they hit the island and one time I saw a house fire. Luckily no one was hurt, but it always leaves me shaken and very upset."

The personal toll that such a gift exacts is why Sandra only talks about her gift after a request for ghost stories or after intense persuasion by family members. "Sometimes it helps to talk about it. Other times it's best to just keep these things to yourself."

While acknowledging that many people are skeptical of her skills, she urges people to keep an open mind about the supernatural and other such phenomena. "I think it's crazy to believe that there's no such thing as ghosts or the after-life. Why do we think that there's no life after death? I like to think there is. I like to think there's more to life than just this. I also know there are things that can never be explained and I tell people that just because you can't understand them doesn't mean they aren't real. I know they are real."

Sandra's story goes back some 20 years, before she moved to Baddeck, and involves the tragic loss of her brother. "As a family, we were very close. The kids grew up as best friends and our parents were wonderful, loving and caring. We had a great childhood, but when my brother grew up he was forced to leave home, like most Cape Bretoners, to search for a job elsewhere."

Eventually Sandra's brother made his way west to the Pacific coast where he found employment on the fishing boats there. "He seemed happy and while we missed him desperately, we were happy for him that he had found something to do. He said the money was good and the other crew members were great to work with. What more could you ask for?"

Sandra says her brother had been gone from Cape Breton for about a year and a half when she had the first premonition. "It was a nice sunny day outside and I was sitting on the front steps, cleaning strawberries for supper that night. I was home alone, but all of a sudden, out of nowhere, I heard my brother calling to me from the kitchen. He said, 'Sandi'—that's what he called me. 'Come here a minute, I want to show you something.' I know it was him. I swear it. I recognize his voice anywhere."

Quickly jumping to her feet, Sandra raced to the kitchen only to find it empty when she got there. "I was spooked. I got cold chills and shook all over. I knew it was him and I knew it was a sign."

That evening, after the supper dishes were cleaned and put away, Sandra was sitting at the kitchen table going over some magazines when she heard a terrible crash from the living room. Thinking one of the children had broken something, she went to where the sound had come from. To her horror, she found a picture of her brother lying face down on the floor. The glass in the frame had shattered into a thousand pieces.

"I kept the picture on a table with all my other pictures. There were probably half a dozen frames on that table. I have no idea how my brother's picture could fall while the others were still there safe and sound. There was an open window close by and the curtains were blowing a bit in a light breeze, but there's no way they could have done it. Why his picture and not the others?"

Why? Because it was another sign, Sandra says.

"I knew what it meant. I went right to the phone and tried to call my brother in B.C. but I couldn't reach him. They told me he had already left for a fishing trip and would be back in three days. I was devastated. I knew what was going to happen."

Sandra told her mother about the premonitions and she too believed that they meant tragedy. That night, Sandra couldn't sleep. She tossed and turned and lay awake thinking about her brother—and waiting for the phone to ring. She knew it was inevitable because these signs were never wrong. Somehow, through all the worry, Sandra finally managed to doze off. While asleep, she dreamed of her brother.

"It was a nightmare. I had just fallen asleep when I saw him. At first he was fine. He looked happy and smiling and strong. But all of a sudden, I saw him floating in the water and his eyes were closed. He wasn't moving. I knew he was going to drown."

Jumping out of bed, Sandra quickly phoned her mother and together they cried. "We knew he was gone. We knew he had drowned."

The next morning, Sandra received the news she reluctantly expected. Someone from the West Coast had phoned her mother with news that her brother had been killed in a freak accident. It seems he had slipped and fallen overboard in a thick fog. The other men on the boat couldn't find him. He was presumed drowned. His body was never recovered.

The End

GHOST HOUSE

Ghost House Books

Look for these volumes in our popular ghost story series:

Ghost Stories of the Maritimes	1-55105-329-2
Canadian Ghost Stories	1-55105-302-0
Even More Ghost Stories of Alberta	1-55105-323-3
More Ghost Stories of Saskatchewan	1-55105-276-8
Ontario Ghost Stories, Vol. I	1-55105-203-2
Haunted Theaters	1-894877-04-7
Ghost Stories of the Rocky Mountains	1-55105-165-6
Ghost Stories of California	1-55105-237-7
Ghost Stories of Hollywood	1-55105-241-5
Ghosts, Werewolves, Witches and Vampires	1-55105-333-0
Ghost Stories of Michigan	1-894877-05-5

Coming soon...

Watch for these upcoming volumes from Ghost House Books:

Ontario Ghost Stories, Vol. II	1-894877-14-4
Campfire Ghost Stories	1-894877-02-0
Ghost Stories of Indiana	1-894877-06-3
Haunted Hotels	1-894877-03-9
A Haunted Country Christmas	1-894877-15-2

Available from your local bookseller.

For more information, contact our customer service department. In the United States, call 1-800-518-3541. In Canada, call 1-800-661-9017.